Fly With GOD

Fly With GOD:
Flight Training 101

Lily Capers Milliner

XULON PRESS

Xulon Press
2301 Lucien Way #415
Maitland, FL 32751
407.339.4217
www.xulonpress.com

© 2020 by Lily Capers Milliner

All rights reserved solely by the author. The author guarantees all contents are original and do not infringe upon the legal rights of any other person or work. No part of this book may be reproduced in any form without the permission of the author. The views expressed in this book are not necessarily those of the publisher.

Unless otherwise indicated, Scripture quotations taken from the King James Version (KJV) – *public domain.*

Scripture quotations taken from the Holy Bible, New International Version (NIV). Copyright © 1973, 1978, 1984, 2011 by Biblica, Inc.™. Used by permission. All rights reserved.

Scripture quotations taken from The Message (MSG). Copyright © 1993, 1994, 1995, 1996, 2000, 2001, 2002. Used by permission of NavPress Publishing Group. Used by permission. All rights reserved.

Scripture quotations taken from the Holy Bible, New Living Translation (NLT). Copyright ©1996, 2004, 2007 by Tyndale House Foundation. Used by permission of Tyndale House Publishers, Inc.

Printed in the United States of America.

ISBN-13: 978-1-6322-1813-1

Thank You, Thank You and Thank You GOD!

First of all, to all the seemingly ordinary people, the true pilots, I met and will meet at church, work, or in my neighborhood that choose to embrace their GOD given talents. I thank you! I am truly grateful for all those supporters GOD provided along this path. May they continue to challenge and cheer for me in the years to come.

Family:

- Mommy-Lucille dearest friend, spiritual mentor, preacher, teacher; never letting me or anyone else forget her Pentecostal teaching invoking the Name of JESUS and "Pleading the Blood of JESUS" on all our efforts
- Daddy—James who loved and encouraged me in all my ups and downs
- Sisters—Gwen Capers Wilson & Valerie Capers Workman for continuously sharpening the book's spiritual applications making it relatable to all GOD's children; along with Carlene Hernandez for being a major part of my Bishop T.D. Jakes International Pastors and Leadership Conference experience & encouragement
- Brothers-in-law (Larry, Tony) and nephews (Marcus, Desmond, RJ) for their love, kindness, patience, perseverance, laughter and most of all joy

Editors who persevered through 100s of drafts and changes knowing in faith, I would finally get this book published:

- Andrea Richards Scott editor, friend and prayer warrior; she negotiated my 1st radio job and brought me to my 1st book expo in New York City

- Rhonda Joseph editor, client, friend and prayer warrior. She drove over 2 hours daily to support my vision for a Christian Youth STEM program

- Valerie Capers Workman editor, coach, baby sister, friend and prayer warrior; let it be said that having a family member as one of your editors ensures you stay faithful to your historical events, no spiritual amnesia

Friends (Sophia Casey, Emma Jackson, Gloria Aparicio-Blackwell, Dianne Betsey, Mary Miller, Briggette Harrington, Tony Jones, Jennifer McIntosh) who have generously been there to shape my story and experiences. They have played a vital role in my road to spiritual growth, integrity and authenticity.

Business Supporters: Delmock Technologies, Inc., Morgan State University, East Coast Chapter of Tuskegee Airmen, and the Docent Program–Smithsonian Institution's National Air and Space Museum [my experience as a docent continues to frame my spiritual conceptualizations].

Social Media Guru: Colin Fraser for his gentle nudge along with the creation of the awesome "Fly High" website and blog.

Table of Contents

Thank You, Thank You and Thank You GOD! v
Introduction ix

Part 1: Packing 1
   Chapter 1: My Facts. 3
   Chapter 2: GOD's Truth 10
   Chapter 3: Forgetting and Forgiving. 16

Part 2: Baggage 25
   Chapter 4: Luggage 27
   Chapter 5: Trash. 37
   Chapter 6: Check-in or Carry-on. 47

Part 3: Baggage Processing 57
   Chapter 7: Defining Baggage Processing 59
   Chapter 8: Contraband: Fear 67
   Chapter 9: Contraband: Disbelief. 78
   Chapter 10: Contraband: Unforgiveness 85
   Chapter 11: Contraband: Slothfulness. 96
   Chapter 12: Contraband: Rebellion 108
   Chapter 13: Other Contraband. 116

Part 4: Terminal 119
   Chapter 14: Check-in. 121
   Chapter 15: Waiting Room 131

Fly With GOD

Part 5: Boarding **149**
    Chapter 16: Reporting for Duty 151
    Chapter 17: Manifest 161

Part 6: Take-off **173**
    Chapter 18: Flight Plan 175
    Chapter 19: Fuel 183
    Chapter 20: Air Traffic Controller (ATC) 193

Part 7: Airborne **205**
    Chapter 21: Understanding Aerodynamics 207
    Chapter 22: Your Engine "The Heart" 226

Bonus Exercises 237
About the Author. 243

Introduction

"The great enemy of truth is very often not the lie—deliberate, contrived and dishonest—but the myth—persistent, persuasive and unrealistic. Too often we hold fast to the clichés of our forebears. We subject all facts to a prefabricated set of interpretations. We enjoy the comfort of opinion without the discomfort of thought." — John Fitzgerald Kennedy

You are the pilot for your life's journey. To *"Fly With GOD"* you must be able to take *"Spiritual Flight"*. Spiritual flight is a way of moving through life in a manner that enables you to follow the course GOD designates for you regardless of your circumstances. It is your ability to hear GOD's voice and act immediately on the knowledge and wisdom you receive. Whether you're at work or cruising the mall for sales, you're making sure to do it GOD's way. *"Fly With GOD"* does not focus on your potential after effects—the better job, better house, the better financial portfolio—but what it does focus on is the best you.

"Fly With GOD" ensures that you will have the joy, peace and contentment that Paul described in the Book of Philippians.[1] It is a constant state of "being above it all." *"Fly With GOD"* provides you with the ability to stay in a place that allows every interaction to be

---

[1] Philippians 4

about GOD—not you—on a daily basis. "Flight Training" is ultimately about teaching you to stay on the course that GOD has charted for your life and the peace you will enjoy by doing things GOD's way.

At this point, you may ask: "Will I be able to achieve my hopes and my dreams if I learn to attain and sustain *spiritual flight*?" The answer to that question is "Yes" and "No." You must understand that when you achieve spiritual flight, you will have the ability to do things that are exceeding abundantly more than you can ever ask or think.[2] GOD prepared a flight plan just for you. The dreams and plans you conceived prior to achieving spiritual flight may not be in line with what GOD prepared for your life. But do not let that sentence discourage you. Rather, you should be encouraged to know that upon achieving spiritual flight, the dreams and plans you conceive will be far greater than you hoped or imagined because the dreams will be inspired by GOD.

Is GOD calling you to fly whether or not you know how? The answer is YES! I believe that you have an innate desire to fly with GOD; you were born to fly but lack the knowledge and preparation to do so. Whether you have almost everything or barely anything, you may still lack the most important thing—the biblical knowledge and preparation needed to receive GOD's vision and fly.

Flight training is for those pilots who yearn to respond to GOD's call to fly; it was developed to give you the tools necessary to Make HIS vision for you a reality. For instance, did you know that too much cargo is the leading cause of aborted flights? Most people don't know the impact of carrying too much luggage on board. That is why *"Flight Training 101"* starts by educating you on the importance of what you "pack" for your spiritual journey. Particularly, how packing incorrectly, that is carrying items GOD has told us to leave or forget, hampers or stops us from lifting off. Flight training helps you analyze your baggage: the types of people, places or

---

[2] Ephesians 3:20

Introduction

things you are carrying; mentally or physically. This self discovery process enables you to lighten your load. When you learn how to discard, pack and process the appropriate items for your flight, you won't exceed the luggage weight limits required to experience a safe and joyful flight.

Once you have the right luggage, you will be ready to face any obstacles in the airport terminal. This is where pilots like you will uncover personal things that only a trip through security and/or a long wait at the boarding gate can reveal. To resolve these challenges, you must embrace the biblical and the personal truths about your life. You must face the "awful truth"–the areas where GOD says you missed the mark. You must also face the awesome truth–the truth about who GOD says you really are–being fearfully and wonderfully made.[3]

After making the necessary adjustments by searching your heart and applying the biblical principles explained in this book, you will be ready to properly determine what and who will stay on your flight manifest. How to complete your flight checklist and the level of communication required between you and GOD (your Air Traffic Controller). As you learn the practical application of biblical principles, you will begin transforming into the person GOD says you are. You will discard the obstacles that keep you grounded. *"Flight Training 101"* can catapult you into the sky!

As you become airborne, you will understand that staying in the air requires just as much work as getting into the air. You will discover that the four forces that affect your flight, once you are airborne, act as counterbalances. The four forces–GOD, Relationship, Work and Ministry–depending on how you utilize them, can cause you to sustain flight, continue soaring or stall. "Flight Training" assists you in understanding how the decisions you make affect these forces. The amount of emphasis you exert upon each of the forces

---

[3] Psalm 139:14

Fly With GOD

work together aerodynamically to initiate, stabilize and/or accelerate flight during your life maneuvers. The effort required to stay airborne must be exerted continuously. The emphasis has to be adjusted and perfected second-by-second in order to obtain and sustain flight.

I'm sure some of you are now questioning the validity of what you just read. Especially the part about all humans being born to fly even if they currently have barely anything. But I'm here to show you that when the LORD "calls" a person to fly, HE always provides the skills and resources needed for every segment of that person's spiritual flight.

2 Timothy 1:9 (KJV)

> *Who... called us with an holy calling, not according to our works, but according to HIS own purpose and grace, which was given us in CHRIST JESUS before the world began...*

As an example, take a look at the biblical background of several good "pilots." Understanding their circumstances may help you understand how your current status bears no relation to your ability to fly with GOD.

Your current circumstances may not be comfortable ...

> *Paul was made blind for three days when he received his call; later stoned; placed under house arrest for two years; ship wrecked; and bitten by a venomous snake. These are just some of the uncomfortable experiences Paul had to face.*

> *Joseph was rebuked by his father and brothers when he received his call; later cast into the pit; as a teenager sold into slavery for 20 pieces of silver;*

falsely accused of sexual harassment; wrongly imprisoned for years; and more...

Your current resume may not match GOD's job description for you ...

> *Peter was a fisherman who became the "rock" of the church*
>
> *Zacchaeus was distained for being a chief tax collector, but JESUS chose him to dine with (seeking and saving).*

Your current money may be low ...

> *Nehemiah, when called to rebuild the wall around Jerusalem, had only a cupbearer's salary; but is later given the King's financial backing and troops to protect him.*
>
> *The Israelites were slaves; but when they left Egypt and did as Moses had told them, they left with silver, gold and clothing.*

You may not know where you're going before you get started ...

> *Abraham, at 75 years old, was told by the LORD to leave his country, his people and his father's household and go to the land that GOD would show him.*
>
> *Moses, at 80 years old, was told by the LORD to go back to Egypt and lead the Hebrew people out of slavery to the Promised Land guided by a pillar of cloud by day and a pillar of fire by night.*

You may be young or old ...

> *Caleb was 85 years old when Joshua gave him an opportunity to change his territorial selection, but*

> he stayed with the hill country which was occupied by a great fortress to drive out the enemy.
>
> _David_ was a teenager (about 17) when he went to battle against Goliath and won.

You may not be a man ...

> _Esther's_ wisdom and humility saved a nation.
>
> _Deborah_ led and won a battle to free the Israelites, who had been cruelly oppressed for 20 years because Barak (Commander) refused to go to war without her.

You may not have a clean police record ...

> _Moses_ killed a man for hitting a Hebrew, hid the body and then remained a fugitive for 40 years.
>
> _David_ made a woman pregnant in an adulterous relationship and to cover it up arranged the murder of her husband.
>
> _Rahab_ was a prostitute who helped to capture Jericho and was a direct ancestor of JESUS.

Where? Where? and where did you read that to fly with GOD would require you to have resources, connections and/or a great resume? When GOD calls you to fly, your past performance, your connections and your current means are all irrelevant to flying. When you are serving CHRIST, your resume is made new. Your abilities seldom equal your purpose. Your resume and resources are only an ingredient in the purpose GOD has for your life. Most of us will find out as we fly that our abilities were only a small portion of what GOD has prepared for us.

Introduction

Disclaimer

This is not a self-help book. This is a GOD-help book. Flight "trainees" following the instructions in this book risk continuous ACTS OF GOD occurring in their life; unpreventable, supernatural events. I am purely a facilitator and am not personally responsible for your blessings—GOD is!

Parachute Required

The training in this book must be used with your "PERSONAL COACH." HE is also referred to in the Book of John as the "COMFORTER"[4] or as the "HOLY SPIRIT."[5] If you don't have a "PERSONAL COACH" and you desire the type of transformation that occurred for the few good *pilots,* I just mentioned, then follow the instructions in Romans 10:9[6] at no additional cost and continue prayerfully reading this book.

What's Next?

If you are still reading this introduction, then I will assume that you have decided to enroll in *"Flight Training 101."* Each chapter builds upon the previous chapter's material, so make sure to answer each question thoughtfully and complete each exercise <u>in writing</u>. Be sure to date all of your entries. You will find that your answers expose the truths and facts about where you are going and/or where you have been. Most of all your answers will illustrate what you need to do to obtain and sustain spiritual flight.

---

[4] John 14:16

[5] John 14:26

[6] That if thou shalt confess with thy mouth the LORD JESUS, and shalt believe in thine heart that GOD hath raised him from the dead, thou shalt be saved.

Part 1: Packing

There's a world of difference between truth and facts. Facts can obscure truth.

Maya Angelou

Chapter 1: My Facts

My PACKING DECISIONS – All the items I decided to initially carry on my journey.

My Personal Story. In 2002, I visited New Orleans, Louisiana with a friend when I received new insight on the importance of *Philippians 3:13-14* to my journey to flight. We prayed for several nights and days. One particular morning GOD woke me up. My heart leaped with HIS words as HE poured out revelation and I received new knowledge. I had to be willing to <u>not</u> pack those items which I had trained myself to believe were valuable. I would be required to forget that those items ever existed as I moved towards GOD's call on my life. To get my attention and help me understand how similar the spiritual realm is to the natural realm when it comes to packing for our journey, GOD shared the following *"packing"* example with me:

> *I'm going on a fantasy trip. One I could never find either the time or money to take. I've been packing for weeks; I have so much baggage. About 200 feet in the distance, I see my plane; brand new with all the first class amenities I could imagine for my trip to an exotic island.*

I notice the door to the plane very slowly beginning to close. Will I make it, I ask myself? I start screaming almost involuntarily, "HOLD THE PLANE!" With the door still closing, I make a very important decision— What will I leave behind?

With suitcases in both hands, trunks and oversized cases stationed at my feet and even more behind me, I'm now thinking, what can I really afford to leave behind? I have a lot of used items in those trunks at my feet; they're old, dirty, worn out and many are even broken. Right now I'm thinking: but they've been with me forever, I can't possibly leave the trunks behind; I might need something from them during my flight, you never know; it looks broken, but "I" can fix it!

The plane's door is still closing so I leave all the baggage at my feet, hoping I can make it without its contents. I begin to jog toward the plane, stumbling across the numerous trunks and oversized suitcases, but the door is still closing. Now I'm struggling to reach the plane, but the baggage in both hands won't let me, I have too many. I feel that I really need what's in those cases. I can't bear to leave them behind. How can I be sure that they will have all that I need in the plane? So I holler one more time "WAAAIITTT!" only to see the door close firmly.

And I WAS LEFT BEHIND.

Leaving Behind. So what did I understand about this revelation that made my heart leap? It was what I found myself writing over the next hour. In those moments, a key to GOD's truth was found and thus a door was opened to me. The key is the word "behind." Before this moment, I did not truly understand what the word behind really meant.

Chapter 1: My Facts

Yes, I was aware of what I considered the big things that I left behind, like when I moved from Binghamton, New York to Washington, DC or when I broke up with my college boyfriend after I found out he was cheating on me. But I had not considered the small things. These small things had continued adding up much like what happens when you have a credit card with exorbitant interest rate. The fees keep compounding unless you eliminate the principal.

I had not understood that a little[7] item has the potential to cause enormous results. I had a glimpse, but I did not have the full revelation of the impact that the statement, "forget those things which are behind" would have on my life until that moment. At that instant, I wished I had only one elephant in the room, but to my dismay there was a herd. Elephants like...

> **Lousy Writing**–*My high school English teacher said, "I'm glad you're pursuing medicine, because you will never be a good writer." Years later, when my proposals won millions and millions of dollars for my clients, I still felt the sting of that teacher's comments. Was winning a fluke? I carried that message for years, even as I wrote this book. Praise GOD, less of that stinging feeling today!*
>
> **Secrets**–*My first boyfriend in high school was with a school bus driver who was in his twenties. I kept our relationship secret from my family and friends until his unfaithfulness led to my first and only fight in school.*
>
> *I kept my second high school boyfriend a secret too; he was even more colorful and older. I met him at my cousin's party. I later learned that he had four children. My parents were heartbroken when my sneaking around was finally exposed and*

---
[7] Galatians 5:9-12

I continued to lie about the relationship. It led to one of the most difficult times in my life—my parents stopped trusting me. My father wouldn't talk to me. He was so hurt and I couldn't fix it. GOD revealed how these kinds of secrets have continued for decades and caused me to be unfaithful to myself.

Wrong Image – *I met my biological mother when I was around five years old – I was in the foster care system. To me, she was truly obese. She was over 6 feet tall and more than 400 pounds. It was then, I believe, I first started questioning my own image. Despite the fact I was at my goal weight—I didn't feel pretty. I believe seeds of not looking good enough were starting to be unleashed. Would I look like her when I grew up?*

I can't remember a time when I talked about liking my body; what I usually felt was ugly. By my 7th birthday, I couldn't take it any longer. My nose was taking over my face and my classmates had no problem confirming it. At 9 years old, my feet were clearly too big; I couldn't find any children's shoes to fit me. Finally, at 11 years old, it was all over. I had become the sum total of my heavily endowed butt and everything else that could possibly be wrong. My sister was constantly teasing me; bringing cups of tea to put on what she called my "shelf." Boys kept on picking on me; which escalated to them hitting my derrière.

As I grew older, it seemed I could only focus on the derogatory comments people made about my body. I was overly sensitive and insecure. I didn't let people know how I felt, but I was hurting all the same. I started developing numerous ways

> *to cope with the pain from crying to eating or my ultimate nemesis—making sure I did everything perfectly along with fixing anything that was wrong. Imperfection was not an option; failure was not an option. Do it perfectly; see it perfectly or not at all. GOD revealed all of these elephants; each a different size, at a different time, but still all my elephants. These elephants were in my baggage!*

My blinders, crazy actions, weird attachments, ugly thoughts, confined dreams and even my limited prayers had shaped my packing decisions. GOD was speaking to my heart; letting me know that all those issues that I was carrying had not been left behind; they were still with me. Not feeling pretty enough, not feeling thin enough, not feeling smart enough or even funny enough had all shaped my packing decisions. I had to somehow personally make up for all those deficits. It is crazy what you will do when you don't feel good enough, no matter what your family tells you.

GOD started revealing my relationships. One by one, HE showed me the packing choice I made. Things like, the first lie a person told me and how I was quick to make excuses for them. GOD even reminded me how HE had warned me the moment I met him or her. HE showed me how I would quench the HOLY SPIRIT and quickly deny the truth; how HE had given me a way out, time and time again, and I chose not to listen until the situation was deplorable.

I knew some of this was true. When I married my ex-husband, the Justice of the Peace asked me to say "I do." At that very moment, I lost my voice, it went from the usual loud tone to being barely audible. I found myself unable to talk above a whisper. I was hardly able to utter the words "I do." Could GOD have given me a bigger sign? The truth is, HE had been trying to talk to me for over 10 months.

Fly With GOD

HE was reminding me how I allowed my ex-husband and so many other people to take advantage of me and take me off GOD's course. HE wanted me to understand how those decisions shaped my packing story. Feelings like success, fun, love, trust, fear, lust and lost had become twisted. I hadn't separated the best from the worst. Everywhere I went, they went. It didn't matter if the items were the best, trash or barely salvageable. They were stuffed in my baggage and went on the journey with me.

GOD required me to take action if I wanted to obtain the prize. I was not sure how, but I was listening. HE would teach me how to pack. I have had many years to listen, think and actually pack since that marvelous event in New Orleans. HE has taught me how to pack and it has been "one-peace" at a time. YES, I mean PEACE!

GOD woke me up for a marvelous revelation. HE gave me a true understanding of leaving behind while pressing forward. This revelation has made all the difference in my journey. I believe that spiritual growth in CHRIST is rooted in our ability to quickly let go of the things that prevent us from pressing toward the prize. Things like hate, jealousy, unforgiveness, lust, pride; I could go on and on, but you get the picture. When we drop those items and forget them we can fly with GOD.

Most of us have experienced at least one **moment** in time when we felt GOD stepped out of heaven, stopped time and spoke directly to us about a promise. Your prize is GOD's promise to you. Forgetting will not matter, if you are unable to take hold of the promise GOD made to you. It does not matter how old the promise is. GOD is not like man—HE keeps HIS promise.[8] Take hold of your prize and fly!

My moment was when HE told me that my hands should be anointed and why. I always thought it was my mouth that had all the anointing. My speaking ability was my gift, my area of comfort.

---

[8] Numbers 23:19

Chapter 1: My Facts

I had the gift of gab. I could really talk. Writing this book was in uncharted territory and dangerous skies. I was in the dark; I NEEDED JESUS to not only see, but to hold on to the prize. Like the Apostle Peter, if I looked at anything but JESUS, I would surely crash. The journey of writing this book has been humbling. I had to learn how to live every precept I wrote about. Memorizing wasn't enough. Even knowledge wasn't enough; only application would work. I had to know and do it for myself. I had to remember and then act on GOD's promise to fly.

This is where I will begin our spiritual flight training; revealing the truth about packing and the consequences of leaving the wrong thing behind. Will it be us and/or our baggage left behind? The choice has always been ours. We just need the knowledge and preparation to move from GOD's teachings into action. Don't rely on your baggage to keep you comfortable. Instead, choose to be comforted by THE COMFORTER. Do not keep old and ineffective items; instead—leave them behind —UNPACK!

Chapter 2: GOD's Truth

Packing or Unpacking – will we let GOD decide?

Awful Truth & Awesome Truth. Understanding the revelation of and the difference between the "awful truth" of who we are and the "awesome truth" of who GOD calls us to be will always lead us to godly packing.

So, how many planes will we be late for or even miss before we are willing to take only what GOD requires? I was making some of the flights, but GOD revealed that morning that I was still missing too many. I was pressing toward the mark, but taking things with me that were part of my awful truth. I didn't need them. I continued to blame the symptoms, my physical body (which was overweight) instead of the cause, my spiritual body (which was also out of shape) for not making those flights. GOD had to reveal an awful truth in order for me to experience the awesome truth of flight. If I could let go of what is not needed on the inside, I would continuously fly with GOD.

So That's My Packing Story. What's Yours?

Chapter 2: God's Truth

I'm learning through the grace of GOD how to share this knowledge with others. What a privilege it is to help you with your packing effort. I would like to offer a prayer for you this moment to help provide you with clarity and strength while you pack!

Precious, Holy FATHER,

May the Word of GOD continue to shape every thought, attitude and action of this child of GOD as they pack for the journey YOU have set before them.

May they always be prepared for the favor YOU placed on them from the beginning of time. Help them to prepare their luggage daily for each and every journey.

May this child of GOD, from this moment through eternity, hunger and thirst after YOUR amazing truth.

Finally, may seeing the awful truth always catapult this servant into the place where YOUR awesome truth for them continually resides!

In JESUS Name – Amen

Are you packing too much or too little for your flight? All trips require you to determine the items you will pack and how you will carry them. Whether it is a trip to your local mall, where you are probably packing just your wallet and keys, or moving into a new home where you might try to pack everything you ever owned. You are always making packing decisions. The quality of those decisions determines your ability to *"Fly with GOD."*

For most journeys, what you decide to take and what you decide to leave is based on where you are going, what you plan to use along the way, and finally your ability to carry them on board. *"Flight Training 101"* will require you to make similar decisions about the items you pack for your spiritual flight. You will have to determine physically and spiritually how not to take too much or

Fly With GOD

too little. You will learn what you should remember, leave, forgive or forget in order to take flight.

When you chose CHRIST, you knowingly started a new journey to follow HIM which compelled you to start packing differently. Most of us, at that time, are told at the minimum the answer to our packing dilemma is to follow the 10 Commandments and be a good Christian. But having gotten that answer you may still need clarity as to how to actually begin applying these principles in order to follow HIM. By now you have found that having a theoretical answer is not enough to compel you to pack properly. You need an answer that teaches you exactly how spiritual packing is done.

In the Book of Matthew, both Peter and Andrew knew the answer to proper packing; they immediately left their nets,[9] followed JESUS. They made it seem so easy to pack light. Peter and Andrew most likely just took the clothes on their backs and whatever they had in their satchels. Few of us have the ability to discard everything we have, so quickly and resolutely the way Peter and Andrew did. Thank GOD few of us are required to do so.

Further in Matthew, we find the rich young man that may resemble us.[10] He follows all the commandments faithfully, but JESUS uncovers this man's secret—HE sees his heart. HE sees that the man's wealth meant everything to him. The importance that wealth held for this man prevented him from being the man that GOD wanted him to be, the one who would fly with HIM.

JESUS knew there was no way this man would fly so long as this weight grounded him. Despite having done some wonderful deeds, his wealth was the one thing he had chosen to pack. JESUS tells him to sell all he has and give it to the poor. The man leaves very sad because he has great wealth and is not willing to unpack it.

---

[9] Matthew 4:20

[10] Matthew 19:22-24

Chapter 2: God's Truth

JESUS reminds us in this passage that the LORD is always looking for what is imbedded (packed deeply) in your heart.

Whether JESUS is telling "wannabe" disciples to "let the dead bury the dead"[11] or a rich man to "sell all," GOD always knows what separates us from HIM. For this man it was his wealth; what will it be for you? Your answer to this question and your subsequent decisions will determine what you will pack for your flight.

Packing can seem to be <u>passive</u> or <u>active</u>, but in actuality it is always active. From the beginning of time, way back with Adam and Eve, GOD has always given mankind the ability to choose.[12] In order to fly with GOD, you must make a decision regarding what you will take with you on your amazing journey. You must also decide what you will leave behind. For many of us, this step of deciding what to pack and what to discard means the difference between being grounded–unable to fly, and actually flying.

In the Bible, GOD has provided a detailed flight plan on how to pack for your flight. A particular passage that helps you understand how to pack for the important missions GOD desires to send you on is found in *Philippians*.

> *Brethren, I count not myself to have apprehended: but this one thing I do, forgetting those things which are behind, and reaching forth unto those things which are before, I press toward the mark for the prize of the high calling of GOD in CHRIST JESUS.*
>
> *Philippians 3:13-14 (KJV)*

In this brief passage, the Apostle Paul provided believers with the blueprint for becoming a packing "aficionado." He shared how he was able to live GOD's way in the present. He understood the truth–that he was not an expert in the Gospel; however; what he

---

[11] Luke 9:59-64

[12] Genesis 1:26-28

Fly With GOD

understood, he applied. He did not focus on the past. He worked on the present and pressed toward the future. He understood that what he chose to pack would directly affect his future success.

Meditation Scriptures

- Galatians 5:7-10 (NIV) You were running a good race. Who cut in on you and kept you from obeying the truth? That kind of persuasion does not come from the one who calls you. "A little yeast works through the whole batch of dough." I am confident in the LORD that you will take no other view.

- 1 Peter 5:6-7 (NIV) Humble yourselves, therefore, under GOD's mighty hand, that HE may lift you up in due time. Cast all your anxiety on him because HE cares for you.

- Matthew 11:30 (New Living Translation)For my yoke is easy to bear, and the burden I give you is light.

Chapter 2: God's Truth

It's truth time! How is your packing proceeding? What do you need to leave behind? What do you need to keep?

Complete "Your Truth Time" exercise below.

Your Truth Time	
Complete each section. Write as much as you can. This is only a snapshot. GOD will reveal much more at your appointed[13] time.	
Awful	**Awesome**
People	People
Place	Place
Things	Things

**Completion Date: ___/ ___/ ___ - 1st Time

** *You will see this form again. Add or subtract information based on revelation and knowledge from the LORD each time. Be sure to date your entries so that you can chart your progress.*

---

[13] Habakkuk 2:3

Chapter 3:
Forgetting and Forgiving

FORGETTING AND FORGIVING – All the items you should NOT carry on your journey.

Forgetting. There is another aspect of Paul's words[14] which GOD revealed. It is the "Forgetting" part. What does it mean *"Forgetting those things that are behind you and to press toward the mark of the high calling?"* The Bible tells us here that the items that we don't pack must be forgotten. It is not enough to leave them behind. We must <u>stop</u> remembering what we have <u>not</u> packed in our suitcases.

There can be no proverbial running to the store once we arrive at our new destination. NO restocking our suitcases with the same contents that we left behind. We need to completely forget about those items which only serve to weigh us down.

Paul wrote this important passage in Philippians to show Christians that we each have a calling and desire to truly reach the prize. He desperately wanted us to know that this will not happen until we leave the unimportant items behind and completely forget them. Forgetting is a verb, it requires us to act, to stay in motion. As Christians, we are to "stop remembering" those items we are

---

[14] Philippians 3:13

Chapter 3: Forgetting And Forgiving

called to leave behind. Our actions of "Forgetting" needs to be done right now—not yesterday or sometime in the future—but right now!

Let me help you understand how critical this is, I'll use my "Pen Approach". Whenever I use to pick up a disposable pen and after scratching it – it still didn't work, I would pick-up another pen and toss the non-working pen back in my purse. Those worthless pens weighed down my purse. I now, make it a habit of throwing out pens which don't work the first time. My purses are much lighter because I have chosen to leave those worthless pens behind. When I make a purchase and the cashier wants to give me one of their disposable pens, I say no thank you. I use the proven pens in my purse and leave their disposable pens behind.

Sometime ago, I realized how much time I wasted trying to use pens that malfunctioned or were untested. The more time I spent trying to fix them, the more time I actually wasted. These pens may have worked in the past, but today they don't. These malfunctioning pens are just like the dysfunctional items alluded to in Philippians.

So Why Not Leave Them Behind Too?

Apostle Paul instructs Christians on their need to continuously apply the Forgetting process. He even humbles himself by letting us know there is a lot he hasn't understood, but this he REALLY, REALLY, gets. He reminds us in the next verse that packing light results in a prize.[15]

You will come closer to the prize from GOD each time you choose to forget the things you are called to leave behind. In the same way you don't value pens that don't work – start not valuing these items. I challenge you to begin the Forgetting process. The way you trash the pens – trash these items.

---

[15] Philippians 3:14

Fly With GOD

Our natural mind may want to remind you of the hurt and pain you have experienced, but your spiritual mind desires you to forget like Paul. In Philippians 3:13-14, he tells as many as will hear, listen and follow the practical applications of packing. The truth is that leaving behind and Forgetting is a moment-by-moment process. The Apostle Paul has become an expert at not remembering what he has left behind. He has come to realize it takes a commitment to "cease to remember."

When you continue to pack everything instead of a prize, you find pain. You may believe that pain and hurt must be remembered and relived to validate the fact that you experienced it. However, the act of remembering is the continual infliction of damage and pain that creates wounds that you cannot heal.

The reaching forward that Paul speaks of is the actual [16]renewing of your mind. In the Book of Romans, he provides you with instructions on the things you should spend time thinking about. He tells you, that you may be transformed by focusing your mind on those things that are "good," "acceptable" and "the perfect will of GOD."

Are you holding onto hurts and pains you have experienced or caused in the past? If so, it's time to leave those experiences behind. The very act of leaving those things behind is an act that JESUS makes available to you if you let HIM. GOD provides you a way out and freedom from those things in your past that keep you on the ground. It is time for you to pack lightly. By listening to the HOLY SPIRIT, you can get rid of trash and begin the Forgetting process.

It is important to note that Forgetting does not mean that you do not acknowledge your past and the events that have led you to where you are at this point in time. Acknowledging and dwelling are two different things. When you acknowledge the ills of your

---

[16] Romans 12:2, And be not conformed to this world: but be ye transformed by the renewing of your mind, that ye may prove what is that good, and acceptable, and perfect, will of GOD.

past, you see them for what they are and understand how your past has contributed to your current status. Dwelling means to continually relive the events and never moving past them. Paul calls us to forget "those things"—whatever they were—to move forward.

The Forgetting process is a foundational element for the believer who is following JESUS CHRIST. Yet, one of the hardest precepts for us to recognize is that the primary component of Forgetting is forgiveness.

Forgiving. There are two types of forgiveness; Personal forgiveness, Forgiving ourselves; and altruistic forgiveness, selflessly Forgiving others. Personal forgiveness can only take place when we have truly repented and the sin is in our past, not our present. Altruistic forgiveness requires that we truly and unconditionally forgive those who are indebted to us due to the wrongs they have committed against us accidentally or on purpose. Most Christians understand that forgiveness is a far more difficult concept to practice than it is to preach.

Let's take a closer look at what it really means to forgive. The kind of Christian "Forgetting" we discussed in the previous paragraphs always comes with its partner "Forgiving." In order to forget, you must first forgive the individual; especially if that person is you! In the LORD's Prayer[17] JESUS says, "forgive us our debts, as we forgive our debtors." Here we are instructed by JESUS to ask for forgiveness of our own debts and to continue to forgive others. A little further in the same passage we are told the consequences of this action. If we are obedient, the blessing is that GOD will also forgive us of our sins. If we are disobedient the curse is that GOD will not forgive us of our sins.

Clearly, the Apostle Paul understood that Forgetting couldn't be accomplished without first Forgiving. Without the activation of those two elements together, he would have continued to create

---

[17] Mathew 6

Fly With GOD

and pack unnecessary baggage. As we follow his life through the New Testament, it is evident by Paul's actions that he packed lightly. He did not have the excess baggage that so many Christians carry with us daily. He applied the truth and successfully stayed in the present; experiencing unspeakable joy.[18] When times seemed harsh on the outside, his declaration was that he could do all things through CHRIST.[19] His many prison experiences still did not stop him from traveling lightly. He did not allow unforgiveness to become part of his baggage. He let nothing separate him from GOD's amazing blessings. He got the PRIZE!

How do we follow the Apostle Paul's example and learn to travel lightly? We begin by not packing certain things. The items that have been forgiven and/or items that need to be forgiven should not be packed. When the LORD forgets our transgressions, those we have sought HIS forgiveness for, HE sets them as far as the east is from the west.[20] That means if the GOD of the universe is not keeping count, we should not keep count either. All four Gospels[21] in the New Testament carry the message that we must forgive. Without forgiveness, we are told, we cannot be forgiven.

I know you're thinking, that's great, but I'm surely not JESUS or even the Apostle Paul. I have to be honest—I have limits to my ability to forgive. How can I forgive and forget all those horrible things that were done to me or I did to others? It is too much to expect me to leave those deep, deep scars behind. How is it possible? The answer lies in our design. We were created in HIS image, thus we have an untapped reservoir of forgiveness in us and the ability to use adversity, just like JESUS did, to triumph over evil. HE

---

[18] Philippians 4:11-13

[19] Philippians 4:13

[20] Psalms 103:12

[21] Matthew 6:12,14-15; Matthew 18:21,35; Mark 11:26; Luke 6:37, 7:4, Luke 23:34

Chapter 3: Forgetting And Forgiving

will allow those scars to become stepping stones to your *"flight"* because GOD has NO limits.

YES, I said scars can be stepping stones if we let them. How you view and use scars will make all the difference in whether you obtain and sustain spiritual flight. The dictionary defines scar in two ways. The initial definition states: it is an indication of damage and/or the mark left by healing an injury; the second definition states: it is a protruding isolated rock; a rocky place on a mountainside. Isn't it great that GOD is using scars not only to heal us, but position us in a higher place than we were before the injury? GOD's plan for spiritual flight has always been about moving HIS people from healing to wholeness. Those scars serve as anchors on the side of the mountain to move us higher and higher.

The transformation from injury to wholeness begins in your mind; this is where we see stumbling blocks changing to stepping stones. It is where you Forget the Pain – Remember the Prize!. You must start believing that GOD has called you to be victorious. No matter what injuries you have had in your past or how bad they were, you must believe that GOD provides a stepping stone for you. I need you to read and absorb into every cell of your being this promise from GOD: "All things work together for good to them that love GOD, to them who are the called according to HIS purpose."[22]. Let that be your stepping stone today and always.

Forget the Pain Remember the Prize!

Those scars, when viewed as indications of damage, do not tell the story of GOD's *awesome truth*. They are things that you believe you need to pack to stay comfortable–or what you have allowed yourself or the world to define as being comfortable. Albert Einstein said it best when he said, *"Reality is merely an illusion, albeit a very persistent one."* Your spiritual reality must be transformed in

---

[22] Romans 8:28

Fly With GOD

order to see your scars the same way GOD views them, as healed and strong enough to be stepping stones to higher heights.

The next exercise may be difficult. I cannot imagine all of the circumstances that have occurred that push loving and kind Christians to hold on to unforgiveness year after year. The Bible talks about wickedness in high places, so I know that the ways to inflict pain and suffering on ourselves and on others are limitless. What I also know, as the Apostle Paul knew, is that our power to stop unforgiveness from festering in our lives is also limitless. Forgiveness allows healing. Healing allows Forgetting. Forgetting allows us to completely move forward, free from the burdens of our past. Finally, freedom allows us to fly with GOD!

Dear FATHER GOD,

I ask you to see the wounds that I am suffering from right now, please touch my heart and mind as only you can. Let nothing interfere with my ability to pack the way you desire me to pack. Take away all stings and stigmas. Change my thoughts so that I can forgive and forget.

Let me write a new chapter full of YOUR mercy and grace, not allowing the ugly memories to separate me from YOUR gift of unspeakable joy and the many victories you have in store for me.

I declare that I will live by the words in Ephesians 4:32, being kind one to another, tenderhearted, forgiving one another, even as GOD for Christ's sake hath forgiven me.

Finally, as a Child of the Most High GOD, I accept the words of 3 John 1:2 I will prosper and be in the best health, even as my soul prospers, by packing under the guidance of the HOLY SPIRIT[23]

In JESUS Name – Amen

---

[23] Adapted from 3 John 1:2

Chapter 3: Forgetting And Forgiving

Meditation Scriptures

- *Matthew 6:9-13 (KJV) The LORD's Prayer Our FATHER which art in heaven, Hallowed be thy name. Thy kingdom come, Thy will be done in earth, as it is in heaven. Give us this day our daily bread. And forgive us our debts, as we forgive our debtors. And lead us not into temptation, but deliver us from evil: for thine is the kingdom, and the power, and the glory, forever. Amen.*

Fly With GOD

Now it is time to reveal your truth. Think about your forgiveness history. Is it one of victory after victory or one of waging war after war unable to forgive? List the items and the day it was revealed to you; victories under the "Forgave" column and your current battles under the "Unforgiven" column.

Unforgiven Examples
LM cheating on me
JJ wrecking my car
SM spreading lies

Forgave Examples
MX not paying back the money he borrowed
JT spreading lies about me
MJ stealing my property

Your Truth Time	
Awful - Unforgiven	**Awesome - Forgave**

Completion Date: ___/ ___/ ___

Congratulations! That must have been a challenge for you to complete. Thank you for digging deep and being honest. Continue to mediate on the scripture and prayer offered in this section to allow all of GOD's blessings to flow.

Part 2: Baggage

No man will swim ashore and take his baggage with him.

— Marcus Annaeus Seneca

Chapter 4:
Luggage

LUGGAGE – All the items of positive value you carry on your journey.

Now that you know about the importance of packing for your journey. You need to know exactly what to pack.

The term baggage throughout this book is defined as anything we take with us on our journey. It is separated into two major categories: Trash and Luggage. The value of the baggage determines how it will be classified. Trash is of negative value whereas Luggage is of positive value. In subsequent chapters, I will show you how to further divide your Luggage into additional categories. [Checked-in Luggage is optional and Carry-on Luggage is a necessity]. These items may change in character along the way; having positive, neutral or negative consequences as you journey towards your take-off destination. They are items which you take ownership of burdens or blessings. Items that have or can shape your spiritual foundation and growth.

An ordinary packer produces flight baggage that can range from trash to treasure, but a Flight-trained packer brings only treasure. So how do you become one of the "Flight-trained" packers? By gaining the biblical knowledge and wisdom necessary to determine the location and value of the items you have included in your

Fly With GOD

baggage. This chapter helps you to thoroughly analyze your baggage—the positive or negative people, places or things you have chosen to pack.

The differences between trash and Luggage in the "natural" can be summed up in the following statements: <u>Trash</u> includes things that are broken, empty, worthless, offensive, filthy, junk, litter, refuse, residue, rubbish, rubble, rummage, scraps, scum, sediment, waste and simply put—garbage. Whereas, <u>Luggage</u> includes bags, cases and containers which hold articles of value; they can be clothing, toiletries, large and small possessions, trip necessities and souvenirs.

> *Now that we know the natural definition of both trash and luggage, how can we explain it in the spiritual realm?*

In the spiritual realm, Luggage is part of your *"Awesome Truth" and is directly related to* who GOD says you are not, and what GOD says you don't need. It includes items for current and future assignments. As we grow spiritually, their value may increase or decrease dramatically, but initially all Luggage has some value (ranging from a grade above trash to certified treasure).

Some of the spiritual characteristics of Luggage are: abiding, accepting, achieving, adoring, aiding, appreciating, assisting, behaving, boosting, championing, comforting, completing, complying, conforming, cultivating, defending, embracing, encouraging, faith, fearlessness, following, forgiving, fostering, fulfilling, giving, guarding, helping, honoring, implementing, loving, nurturing, obeying, peace, performing, pleasing, praising, promoting, resisting, reverencing, serving, submitting, supporting, surrendering, treasuring, upholding and worshipping. As you learn to carry these worthwhile items in a godly way, you will begin to fly higher and higher toward the person GOD intended you to be.

Chapter 4: Luggage

At the beginning of your journey, you may have a lot of "just in case this happens" Luggage. As you progress towards your destination, some of these items may work only marginally and might have to be adapted or disposed of in order to support the person you are becoming.

In the spiritual realm, trash is part of our *"Awful Truth"* and is directly related to who GOD says you are, <u>not</u> and what GOD says you <u>don't</u> need. It is all the items that are no longer effective in promoting your spiritual growth. Trash is your worthless thoughts, actions and/or desires that do not line up with what GOD is calling you to be.

Some of the spiritual characteristics of trash are: fear, grumbling, pain, abuse, back-stabbing, bad-mouthing, bashing, belittling, berating, cutting down, defaming, dump on, insulting, knocking, nagging, offending, oppressing, persecuting, picking on, putting down, reviling, ruining, slapping, smearing, swear at, tearing apart, shooting down, striking, violating–you get the idea. As you learn to discard these worthless items, you will begin to fly higher and higher towards the person GOD intended you to be.

Our trash may even represent things that we are now ashamed of; items that we insist on holding on to and serve to fill a hole inside of us. In utilizing our trash to fill the voids in our lives, we allow ourselves to remain grounded by the past, unable to achieve Spiritual Flight.

This type of shame-ridden trash is the kind you sneak into your baggage for emergency purposes. As soon as you even suspect that you may be approaching take off, you pull this trash out of your baggage to sabotage your growth. The shameful trash you carry may include prescription, over-the-counter or illegal drugs, food, alcohol, casual sex, gambling, gossiping and work.

Trash vs. Luggage: Scanning Your Baggage to Reveal the Difference. So how do you determine the difference between trash and

Fly With GOD

Luggage in the spiritual realm? Let's take a close look at someone from the Bible who had a successful track record of discarding trash and carrying his Luggage.

In the first chapter of the book of Nehemiah, we find Nehemiah preparing to Fly. He had just found out that the Jews who had returned from exile were not only having problems, but the wall around Jerusalem still had not been rebuilt.

Nehemiah, with a heavy heart, took this sorrowful news to the LORD. He fasted and prayed, seeking direction from GOD on what he should pack for his trip. He received guidance from GOD; favor of his boss the king (royal documents) which allowed him to obtain the resources necessary to take off.

Notice! Nehemiah did not take a lot of baggage with him. He only took his treasure: from the king—a few documents along with officers and their army; from the LORD—HIS Word[24]. He acquired the additional resources once in flight; pressing towards GOD's calling for his life.

Nehemiah Brings His Carry-On Luggage. Carry-on Luggage is defined as those items which are of such necessity they must be at your disposal at a moment's notice. For the Christian, carry-on Luggage is the baggage which GOD has determined you need for your journey. Often, the resources GOD requires you to pack seem meager; to the contrary, they are all you need for your mission. Our logical mindset must be disengaged for us to allow the HOLY SPIRIT to determine our baggage; only when we allow this to take place will we really fly high.

I was reminded of this fact several years ago, when I experienced the power of packing only my carry-on Luggage. I had registered for a conference which I really did not want to attend. I hadn't had time to prepare and barely knew how to get there, but I felt GOD

---

[24] Nehemiah 2:9

Chapter 4: Luggage

nudging me to go anyway. With a lot of resistance, I packed my business cards, put on a happy face and went.

When I arrived at this posh event, I only knew one person and he was way up front. Hours went by with one distinguished speaker after another, sharing how the Department of Homeland Security would be conducting business in the future. As I sat there feeling like the least among the attendees, I wondered why GOD wanted me there. I met some nice men from a Fortune 500 company but that didn't seem to be the reason.

After lunch, as I went into the restroom, I noticed someone who seemed like she was talking about me. When I exited, she asked me if I would be willing to be interviewed for a national television network about the conference. She created a wonderful segment with me as the centerpiece; all of this because I followed the LORD's orders.

All I took was my business cards, but it was enough. I went—even though I didn't feel I was ready. I often wonder how much we miss when GOD chooses us, but we choose to wait for more baggage. Listening to GOD's voice allows us to take only the necessities for the trip HE has planned for us.

So back to Nehemiah,—what kind of Luggage did he bring and why? Only carry-on Luggage! This is GOD Luggage; no trash—just treasure. He had barely any Luggage to speak of. He had been given a major mission from GOD, one that the Israelites had not been able to complete for 70 years. He was leaving what we might view as job security to follow HIS call and accomplish the task.

You might ask, "Why didn't Nehemiah pack much more than a few letters and his faith[25]?" For many of us, the fact that he had an escort, the blessing of the king, and GOD's directive to go— would still not be enough. Our thoughts would be on all the work

---

[25] Nehemiah 2:7-9

Fly With GOD

Nehemiah had ahead of him to accomplish in hostile territory with no cash reserves or supplies. There are some Christians who would have considered themselves unprepared for the flight because they believe lots of baggage equals preparation; but GOD said Nehemiah had everything he needed to Spiritually Fly!

In fact, Nehemiah understood the critical nature of his mission; that carrying even one unnecessary item would weigh him down and render him unable to achieve his mission. When you have your carry-on Luggage at your disposal, you don't need anything else. In fact, you shouldn't take anything else.

So whose report about your baggage will you believe? [26]

Many of us would find our flights exceeding the weight limit if we packed resting on our own understanding for task we are to complete each day. When we finally got all we thought we needed, we would desperately try to take off, but somehow we would be unable to ascend. To us, prepared means having every possible earthly material available before we begin the journey; even if it means delaying the flight for a lifetime or for 40 years. That's exactly what the children of Israel did in the desert when they decided not to believe Caleb and Joshua's report that GOD would give them power to possess the occupied land of Canaan[27].

This inability to obtain lift-off is because of what we have not gotten rid of in our life: the false security blankets, the things we have leaned on instead of faith in GOD. We have not believed GOD's message—as HE reminds us time and time again that we need only HIM. We have not left the trash behind and taken only the treasure as Nehemiah did.

As we finally come to the realization, we're wrong about the amount of baggage we need to fly. GOD waits patiently! As we

---

[26] Numbers 13:30

[27] Numbers 13

Chapter 4: Luggage

understand, we only need what HE tells us we need, and that everything else is just trash.

YES, GOD anticipates some Luggage. HE knows that we, being human, are not capable of discarding "everything," but some of the things we insist on carrying are so ungodly. HE will not allow us to soar to new heights until we are willing to leave that trash behind.

At this point, you may wonder why GOD allows so many people to achieve what the natural world defines as great success when they obviously have not discarded their trash; however, you must not confuse material success with "Spiritual Flight." As I explained earlier, material success is separate and distinct from "Spiritual Flight." Having an abundance of costly goods is not proof that a person has achieved the inner peace that comes from living the way GOD wants one to live—though it can be the very pleasant by-product of doing so.

At this point, you may also ask why you have gotten as far as you have in your marriage, your career, your life, when you know that, as a Christian, you are not even close to being the person GOD wants you to be. You know very well that you are carrying a lot of trash and you may even secretly wonder how far GOD is going to let you get before HE requires you to discard the trash that you insist on lugging around each day. It is important for you to know that the only reason some of us even make lift off is because of HIS mercy and grace. In the spiritual realm, GOD allows a kind of Spiritual 747[28] to exist.

This Spiritual 747 is GOD's permissive[29] will. This is the will resulting from our fleshly desires. Our flesh will cause us to pursue an imperfect plan—one very different from GOD's perfect plan, HIS perfect

---

[28] Boeing 747 also known as the jumbo jet (from AviationExplore.com (http://www.aviationexplorer.com/747_facts.htm) 2nd largest passenger airliner after the Airbus A380.

[29] GOD is lenient because of his mercy and grace

Fly With GOD

will for us to fly solo with HIM. When we earnestly pray, pulling on GOD to approve our limited plan; when HE finally relents to all our pleading—saying YES, knowing it is not HIS best plan for us, GOD's act of permitting is HIS permissive will.

Our Spiritual 747 will allow us to take off, but the baggage and passengers on board will end up dictating our journey instead of the LORD. To understand this better, we need only look at Saul's appointment as king of Israel. In the Old Testament, the Prophet Samuel[30] begrudgingly appointed Saul as king over Israel after the people continued to beg the LORD. GOD did not desire to give Israel a king. HIS perfect will was to fellowship with them personally for them to experience, firsthand, pure love; but they wanted to communicate through a king (Saul), like all the other nations around them. So, GOD allowed HIS permissive will to take place and HE gave them Saul as their king. King Saul later turned out to be a wicked king, eventually causing the people to greatly suffer.

Because we do not have the omnipresent view that GOD has, we are unable to see what GOD sees. That's why it is important that GOD's will be done. In the natural realm, the 747 is one of the largest passenger aircrafts in commercial service. But remember, we are not in commercial service; GOD's will is for private duty (GOD's perfect will).

The journey has been designed for just you and HIM to fly solo, not all this baggage you are carrying. GOD's perfect will demands that sooner or later in your journey you will be in a plane at least as fast as the SR-71[31] (three times the speed of sound). GOD wants you to fly at least that fast. To accomplish this, you will have to

---

[30] 1 Samuel 8-10

[31] From CNN.com SCI-TECH (http://archives.cnn.com/2001/TECH/science/06/02/fastestplane/); which holds the title as the fastest air-breathing plane in the world with a speed slightly above Mach 3 (Mach -a measure of speed relative to the speed of sound, thus three times the speed of sound)

Chapter 4: Luggage

lighten your load by getting rid of all that trash and this will take prayer without ceasing[32].

Dear FATHER GOD,

I know YOU are a revealer of secrets. There is nothing which can be hidden from YOU. I ask YOU to give me the wisdom and strength to let go of my heavy loads.

Allow me, upon YOUR revelation, to have the courage to let it go and let YOUR marvelous light in.

Help me replace each item with the treasure YOU provide!

In JESUS Name – Amen

Meditation Scripture

- *1 Corinthians 13:12 (King James Version (KJV)) For now we see through a glass, darkly; but then face to face: now I know in part; but then shall I know even as also I am known.*

---

[32] 1 Thessalonians 5:17

Fly With GOD

Truth Time

Based on the definitions of "Trash" and "Luggage," what is GOD revealing to you right now about your baggage? How would you characterize some of the key people in your life, your emotions, your behaviors, your possessions, your memories? Please share your thoughts below:

Your Truth Time		
Trash		**Luggage**
	People	
	Emotions	
	Behaviors	
	Things	
	Other	

Completion Date: ___/___/___

Chapter 5:
Trash

TRASH – All the items of negative value you carry on your journey.

Take a look at the items you listed as "Trash". Trash is deadweight in our baggage that is negative in value and serves to lie or mislead us about our birthright to receive GOD's best. They are the past or current bad experiences that have occurred during our journey through life. They are actions or thoughts that are done to us or we did to ourselves and their consequences. Things like too much work, food, drugs, sex or anything else like that. Trash includes items that we insisted on buying even though we <u>knew that we could not afford them</u>.

This Trash creates a barrier separating you from GOD's "Awesome Truth" about how you should fly. It must be unpacked in order for GOD's best to be purposed in your heart.

Be honest with yourself. If you had the ability to do so, how good would it feel to get rid of the trash you are carrying?

Dumping the Trash. So how do we identify the Trash and unpack it, so we can experience GOD's best? How do you know whether you listed <u>all</u> of the Trash in *"Your Truth Time"* exercise? In order to truly understand what Trash is, Christians first need to know the "Awful Truth" about what Trash looks and smells like.

The challenge for most Christians is that their radar is off. They cannot see or smell their own Trash. Ironically, many Christians find it very easy to identify the Trash their fellow Christians carry. JESUS warned us of the danger of this selective vision when HE cautioned us about insisting on removing the spec from someone's eye while ignoring the log protruding from our own.[33]

To their ultimate detriment, many Christians do not realize that something is really Trash until the stench of decay becomes so strong that it can no longer be ignored. By this time, the negative consequences of carrying the Trash cannot be avoided and the Christian must pray for deliverance. This could have been avoided by getting rid of the Trash sooner.

Galatians[34] provides spiritual guidelines for determining what Trash is: *"Now the works of the flesh are manifest, which are these; Adultery, fornication, uncleanness, lasciviousness, idolatry, witchcraft, hatred, variance, emulations, wrath, strife, sedition, heresies, envying, murders, drunkenness, reveling ..."* These negative qualities must quickly be unpacked. They represent dead things we are carrying or caring for. The Word tells us GOD has given us the ability to choose life or death, blessings or curses. HE wants us to unpack the Trash and choose life.[35]

Choose or Lose. The act of identifying and unpacking Trash is a voluntary act. One must "choose" to do so. Joshua understood how important our choices[36] are to whether we stay in bondage or receive our inheritance and fly. When we first notice him in the

---

[33] Matthew 7:3-5

[34] Galatians 5:19-21

[35] Deuteronomy 30:19

[36] Joshua 24:15-28

Bible, he is urging his fellow Israelites to choose [37]Faith instead of Fear. Then again when Moses directed him to choose the men he would lead in their first battle in the desert. It is in this battle that he defeats the Amalekites.[38] Joshua continues on to win the battle of Jericho[39] with his praise team and is responsible for these famous words about choices:

> *And if it seem evil unto you to serve the LORD, choose you this day whom ye will serve; whether the gods which your fathers served that were on the other side of the flood, or the gods of the Amorites, in whose land ye dwell: <u>but as for me and my house, we will serve the LORD</u>.*[40]

Joshua proved time and time again how your choices determine your present and future journeys. To stay in bondage or receive your inheritance was a choice GOD gave to the Hebrew children; that same choice is still yours today. Whether it is in the spiritual or the natural; choosing a certain job or career path; choosing whether to begin each day in prayer—GOD has given you the ability to choose your destiny. Your destiny is therefore determined, in part, by what you choose to take with you on life's journey.

Flight training is about a continual commitment to choose abundant life; by unpacking the Trash and then dumping; not straightening it up, not jury-rigging it so it can work. Digging up and taking out the Trash will require you to go deep into your heart and eliminate anything which does not line up with the Word of GOD. Only when you dig deep and work on those important items will you actually be moving toward your ultimate destination, GOD's call on your life.

---

[37] Numbers 14:5-9

[38] Exodus 17:9

[39] Joshua 5:13-15

[40] Joshua 24:15

Fly With GOD

To do this, you need to take each item and assess the value of the item in your life; you need to hold it up to the SON–light. Assessing the truth requires the past, present and future to be completely uncovered; to let in all the SON–light.

The truth about who you were, what you are and what you will allow GOD to do, moves you into your calling. You may have a history much like the woman who touched the hem[41] of JESUS garment; she was frustrated and an outcast. You may have suffered for years, going from place-to-place, church-to-church, doctor-to-doctor, relationship-to-relationship and still not experienced the release from your Trash until you finally touched JESUS.

One of my favorite instructions on how to unpack our Trash comes from 2 Timothy 2:15, where we are told to *"Study to shew thyself approved unto GOD, a workman that needeth not to be ashamed, rightly dividing the Word of truth."* We will only become unencumbered by the Trash when we are able to rightly divide the truth; the truth of knowing that we are joint heirs to a heavenly kingdom. Our ability to touch more and more of GOD will allow the truth to flow in every aspect of our lives–driving out the Trash.

If you are battered and abused or the batterer and abuser, where in the Bible did you read that choosing this existence is preferable? If you are rightly dividing the Word of truth, you know GOD wants, above all things, for you to prosper even as your soul prospers.[42]

The truth about this Word of GOD is not that it is just meant to signify monetary prosperity. Prosperity means choosing whatsoever is good.[43] Have you tricked yourself into believing that <u>any</u> good can come from mental and physical abuse? Have you allowed lies such as "it's better to keep the family together" or "the children

---

[41] Matthew 9:20

[42] 3 John 1:2

[43] 3 John 1:11, Romans 16:19, Micah 6:8, James 2:14, Romans 12:2

Chapter 5: Trash

need a father" or "he doesn't mean it" or "I just blow up sometimes" to justify holding on to the Trash of abuse?

How about your children's education? Are you measuring the educational impact of parents or just teachers? By the time you realized the "great school" you slaved to afford wasn't all that different from the "good school" it might be too late. If your job only allows you to see your children at bedtime and on the weekends, where in the Bible did you read choosing this existence is GOD's best?

If you are "rightly dividing the Word of truth," you know that neither you nor your children can ever regain the time you gave to that job. A "good school" with more mommy and daddy time always produces more treasure and less Trash. Come on—Dig deep.

Dumping. Our spiritual inventory needs to come under thorough scrutiny to determine what needs to be unpacked and then cleaned out. To convey this process as vividly as possible, I started thinking about how similar cleaning the refrigerator is to cleaning out our spirit and how some folks accomplish the task:

> *They open their refrigerator and smell something strange; but for them it is not reeking yet; they are so busy with everything else; they make a choice to leave it in the refrigerator until they have more time to dump it.*
>
> *In the meantime, that trash continues to decay; the only difference now is that it is infecting the fresh items in the refrigerator. As they open the door day after day, they notice the odor is getting stronger and stronger; everything is starting to take on a toxic smell. It is starting to get very disgusting in there.*
>
> *When people come by their home, they are afraid to open the refrigerator because of the stench that fills the room when they open it.*

Fly With GOD

> *Finally, they are unable to use the refrigerator because of the trash that has piled up. So one day, they put on their gloves, face mask, and start dumping everything in the trash.*
>
> *They sanitize it and begin again; this time hopefully remembering that the strange smell was the first sign of their problem.*

Can you see a striking resemblance to the things in your life that you are choosing to ignore? Then you have Trash; things in your life that you are unwilling to part with despite the fact they no longer serve their purpose.

The only way you finally get rid of the person, place or thing is when some crisis occurs causing you to blow up and completely discard it. So many relationships, jobs and situations end like this. The refrigerator, just like our spirit, stores food that is supposed to nourish and replenish our bodies, not harm them. Our spirit should be storing the qualities of the "Fruit of the Spirit,"[44] not those toxins listed on the previous pages.

> *Most of us would never let our refrigerator get that bad, so why do we let our spirit get so bad?*

For the average Christian, I believe our sense of smell can be so deceiving to our spirit that we allow things to appear as if they smell good or maybe we allow the things that smell great to mask the things which are rotten. To identify and dump the spiritual Trash, we must start by not letting our great smells camouflage the stinking Trash.

Those negative qualities Galatians talks about don't just show up in full force. They come in a little at a time, hoping to come in under your smell radar. It might be that twinge of jealousy you experienced when a co-worker received a promotion or that dispute you had with your neighbor. It smelled a little strange, but for most of

---
[44] Galatians 5:22-23

us that behavior didn't reek of sin yet. It was self-righteous anger. Everyone told us how right we were; we had been mistreated. We were so busy being right we didn't notice how great its impact was in establishing a foothold for more situations like that to occur.

This was how we first began packing Trash, a little at a time. That Trash continues to decay; envy, hatred and backbiting showed up too, infecting the once healthy spirit. Just like that refrigerator example, we and other folks start noticing a faint odor. Maybe folks are starting to ask us what's wrong, or worse yet, we have let this Trash remain so long that people no longer mention it; instead, they just stay away or placate us. Now, we stink so much that we become immune to the smell as the decay continues to infect everything we touch.

How do we clear our nostrils and bring back the sweet smell?

The prophet Isaiah tells us: *"Butter and honey shall he eat, that he may know to refuse the evil, and choose the good.*[45]*"* He is giving us a framework as to how we will be able to smell sin. If the "Fruit of the Spirit "[46] is love, joy, peace, longsuffering, gentleness, goodness, faith, meekness, temperance and that is our benchmark for good, then anything that does not taste like that will be dumped.

Much like our refrigerator, we have to make a decision; if the item does not smell fresh, if it does not taste good anymore, we need to get rid of it NOW!

What other sweet smells do we have in our life that enable us to mask the stench that is festering. Is it the wife-batterer (stench) that is also a "loving" father and/or "good" provider (sweet)? Is it the six-figure job (sweet) that requires us to be away from your family for eighty hours per week (stench)? Is it the "great" mother (sweet) who is also an adulterous wife (stench)? Is it the friend we

---

[45] Isaiah 7:15

[46] Galatians 5:22-23

Fly With GOD

can count on to always listen to your problems (sweet) who tells us to stop trying it is okay to stay in our mess (stench)?

In order to Fly we must see and smell Trash for what it is. See the truth in the items we are carrying. Items are either Trash or luggage,[47] they cannot be both at the same time–the Trash has got to go.

GOD wants to give us fresh food each and every day. HE wants to take us back to the Garden of Eden where all is right. I just saw a visual of what GOD wants to do in my life and yours. HE wants us to see our lives as those refrigerators I mentioned earlier, but this time HE wants us to unplug them.

HE has the best food for us. The food inside of them is becoming more and more rancid. HE wants us to reach in and pull out every item. Each item is in a container or wrapped in something that makes it hard to see. It is up to us whether we dispose of it quickly or try to ascertain what is in the package.

> *Will we try to unwrap it to see what's inside or will we trust our spiritual nose and just eliminate it? Or will we, despite the smell, try to find some piece of the product that we feel is still salvageable and force it to work? Will we scavenge through the garbage to find something of substance or will we finally choose to eat from the King's table?*

There is always something you will want to hold on to despite the fact it no longer works or tastes the way it was designed. This is where trusted spiritual advisors and friends are needed to help you dump it. I have had to engage an accountability partner for a few of these items I was unwilling to let go. This person was responsible for reminding me that I needed to unpack that item and move on, no matter how I thought I could adapt to it. I had

---

[47] 1 John 1:5-7

to remind myself that holding onto the Trash would never allow me to Fly.

BEWARE: Trash not only tries to masquerade as luggage; but has the additional property of being able to re-materialize based on a mid-air event. These events may represent areas in your life that you thought you were delivered from; hidden scars and/or new hurts which occur as you fly. You will need to be constantly vigilant to insure that if and when trash materializes in mid-air you are swift to eradicate it.

Finally, if you are to Fly high, the Trash must first go out! Before checking your baggage on the plane, start checking the conditions of acceptance with JESUS. It is time to ensure the items you intend to take on a flight are not classified as Dangerous Goods. Start leaving the Trash and cleaving to the promise GOD has for you, which is to Fly.

Stop trying to save it before it spoils; it already has. Stop saying it wasn't as bad as you thought it was–it really was that bad. Furthermore, stop throwing the item away and replacing it with a similar item for fear you can't live without it. It's time to have the confidence that your future is not based on Trash. Stop living in the garbage dump; even homeless people won't go through the Trash for food when they don't have to.

Smell the fresh food the FATHER in Heaven gives us daily!

Dear GOD,

Change my smell. Allow me to smell trash even when the enemy is trying to deceive me.

*Once I smell trash,
give me the courage to unpack it then quickly dump it.*

In JESUS Name – Amen

Fly With GOD

Meditation Scriptures

- *Galatians 5:22-23 (KJV) But the fruit of the Spirit is love, joy, peace, longsuffering, gentleness, goodness, faith, meekness, temperance: against such there is no law.*

After meditating on the above scriptures, list your behaviors. The behaviors which are directly opposite to the category listed in the "Fruit of the Spirit" column. The behaviors you now would consider trash. (For example if you hate someone – you would write hate on the "love" row under the opposite behaviors column.)

Fruit of the Spirit	*Your Truth Time* Opposite Behaviors
Love	
Joy	
Peace	
Longsuffering	
Gentleness	
Goodness	
Faith	
Meekness	
Temperance	

Completion Date: ___/ ___/ ___

Chapter 6:
Check-in or Carry-on

CHECK-IN OR CARRY-ON: Is determined by whether you need the luggage immediately or much later in your journey.

As discussed earlier in this book, luggage in the spiritual realm makes up shades of our *"Awesome Truth."* It has some value ranging from minimal to great. Check-in Luggage is good but <u>not</u> GOD's best, whereas Carry-on Luggage is GOD's best. In the Book of Matthew, JESUS gives us a detailed packing list for traveling light for our journey. HE provides us with this Baggage Information Sheet for the expert pilot:

> *JESUS said in Matthew,*[48] *"Therefore I say unto you, Take no thought for your life, what ye shall eat, or what ye shall drink; nor yet for your body, what ye shall put on. Is not the life more than meat, and the body than raiment? Behold the fowls of the air: for they sow not, neither do they reap, nor gather into barns; yet your heavenly FATHER feedeth them. Are ye not much better than they? Which of you by taking thought can add one cubit unto his stature?*

---

[48] Mathew 6:25-34

Fly With GOD

> *And why take ye thought for raiment? Consider the lilies of the field, how they grow; they toil not, neither do they spin: And yet I say unto you, That even Solomon in all his glory was not arrayed like one of these. Wherefore, if GOD so clothe the grass of the field, which today is, and tomorrow is cast into the oven, shall HE not much more clothe you, O ye of little faith? Therefore take no thought, saying, What shall we eat? or, What shall we drink? or, Wherewithal shall we be clothed? (For after all these things do the Gentiles seek:) for your heavenly FATHER knoweth that ye have need of all these things.*
>
> *But seek ye first the kingdom of GOD, and HIS righteousness; and all these things shall be added unto you. Take therefore no thought for the morrow: for the morrow shall take thought for the things of itself. Sufficient unto the day is the evil thereof."*

Take no thought about your luggage—for what you will eat, drink and wear, because GOD has taken care of the luggage for the least ones on earth, so you know HE will take care of yours. If HE has done all this for the least, why don't we have the faith to believe HE will take care of what HE calls HIS treasure[49]—US!

We need only look at our past history to support the fact that worry never changed any outcomes for the better. If anything, it often made it worst–illness, anger, premature aging and so on. GOD has always known exactly what we need in our luggage. HE instructs us, in this passage from Matthew, not to pay attention to packing, but instead to seek daily the Kingdom of GOD and HIS righteousness. As we accomplish this task, the HOLY SPIRIT personally instructs us on how to pack our luggage.

---

[49] Exodus 19:5, Deuteronomy 14:2

Chapter 6: Check-in Or Carry-on

Only GOD knows[50] what is deep in our hearts:[51] the treasure and/or the trash. HE knows where the trash is—the best time and most importantly, the best way to dispose of it. By seeking GOD's Kingdom first, we allow HIM to work on our luggage at the proper time—while we work on HIS plan for us. Seeking the Kingdom of GOD is not an easy task. We must listen daily and act on what GOD is telling us personally to accomplish.

The disposal process is also critical; the trash needs to be treated much like any infestation problem. I was watching the news last week and it was cautioning the public about bed bugs. As I heard the expert discuss the dangers of improper disposal, I realized it was the same way with our trash. The fact is that you must be very careful when and how you eradicate it.

The expert talked about how putting infected items out for pick-up may actually be spreading the bugs to the community. He provided the viewers specific details how to detect, eliminate, and eradicate these bugs. He noted the procedure was two-fold: to eliminate them in the home and make sure they did not spread into the community (potentially causing re-infestation).

The task of making sure our trash does not continue to affect ourselves or others can seem to be an overwhelming task if we begin to look at our past and/or our future, but that is why verse 34 tells us it is sufficient to stay in today. If we feel weary along the way, doubting if that will be enough; we need only to think about Philippians 1:6 for peace and strength, as HE reminds us to *"Be confident of this very thing, that HE which hath begun a good work in you will perform it until the day of JESUS CHRIST."* This should restore your confidence in the "HOLY SPIRIT" in you.

Your ability to pack better and better for each journey you take with the LORD, rests solely on the spirit that works in you, not in

---

[50] Romans 8:27-28

[51] Jeremiah 17:8-10

Fly With GOD

your mother or father, your preacher, your friends, the church you attend or even your will power; but HIS power to help you pack only treasure for your journey.

The real difficulty each of us faces in determining our baggage composition is ourselves; we want to pack what we believe we need. Many of us have become seasoned professionals when it comes to packing the wrong items, but complete novices in packing the right items. Pride has allowed us to believe a man-made safety net is something righteous and faithful. [52] Too often this kind of packing has nothing to do with strengthening our GOD-faith; to the contrary, it leaves little room for what GOD has declared valuable. Somehow, we have chosen to take the lesser quality items with us as our storm repellants. In reality, these used, borrowed, abused, shoddy, cut-rate items are unable to withstand the storms that will come our way.

I believe packing is all about godly preparation and yielding to JESUS CHRIST. A relationship with the LORD requires reading and applying the Word of GOD in spirit and body. It also requires that your ears be tender enough to hear HIS voice and that your feet be swift enough to obey HIS command. Not everything needed on your journey will be in your luggage in the initial pre-board phase. But GOD will make sure you have all that you need when you need it.

The Book of Philippians explains luggage best by saying: "...whatsoever things are true, whatsoever things are honest, whatsoever things are just, whatsoever things are pure, whatsoever things are lovely, whatsoever things are of good report; if there be any virtue, and if there be any praise, think on these things[53]." We are instructed to focus on the things of virtue, but often the things of virtue come with things that are Good, but not GOD's Best for us.

---

[52] 2 Samuel 24 David counts the fighting men

[53] Philippians 4:8

Chapter 6: Check-in Or Carry-on

To determine whether luggage is a Check-in or a Carry-on item requires us to analyze whether the item is Good or GOD's Best.

Checked-in Luggage (Good but not GOD's Best). This is luggage that has a form of godliness. Things we should do, but not to the excess like cleaning, working, sleeping, eating, fellowship and so on. Items we bring with us to be done in moderation making sure to line them up with the Word of GOD.

Let's talk about relationships. They are great examples of Check-in Luggage. They are often very Good, but sometimes not GOD's Best. What do I mean by that? Your Christian mentors, friends, associates are all men and women. They are not perfect; they all have things in their life that GOD is working on, but they also have some wonderful traits that GOD has personally matured and may desire that they share with you.

In the Old Testament, the Prophet Samuel[54] is begged by Israel to appoint a king like all the other nations. GOD did not desire to give them a king, HE wanted to fellowship with them personally; for them to experience firsthand, pure love. But they wanted to communicate through a king. So GOD instructed Samuel to anoint Saul as leader over Israel.[55]

When King Saul became tired of being righteous–submitting to GOD,[56] he revealed his true nature. By the time he did this, it was too late for Israel; they suffered the consequences of the lesser choice. He went from being considered by Israel to be treasure to finally being trash. Samuel knew GOD was offering Israel the best and they were choosing less.

Check-in Luggage may provide some happiness, but the LORD wants to fill you with so much joy that you will stop focusing on

---

[54] 1 Samuel 8

[55] 1 Samuel 9:15

[56] 1 Samuel 15:11

Fly With GOD

what you don't have and FLY. The LORD wants to give you the portion HE was ready to give Israel that day by seeking first HIS Kingdom—HIMSELF—the carry-on luggage.

Carry-on Luggage (GOD's Best). Our Treasure: Our Carry-on Luggage holds the gift of HIS intimacy and fellowship; the kind which touches and cleanses us; the kind which discards all unnecessary baggage; the blessing which make us rich and adds no sorrow[57]. This luggage is considered part of our tactical and/or strategic resources and should be closely guarded. If it were lost, it would weaken our mission. It is not only what we are wearing on the plane, but the luggage we can't live without.

The weapons of warfare are the tactical and strategic resources we bring onboard. The weapons needed to fight the adversary. It is the power of that arsenal which makes all the difference between deliverance and defeat. Mark 9:14-29 is the story of defeat and then deliverance. A father brings his ill son to the disciples for healing. The disciples are unable to drive out the evil spirit. After JESUS heals him, HE tells the disciples prayer and fasting are the weapons needed to drive out this kind of spirit.[58]

Carry-on items represent the baggage that we don't want to be separated from at anytime, in case of a surprise attack. These are valuable items that you will need constantly. In the natural world it might include guns, ammunition, food, money, gas mask, parachute, maps and toiletries. In the spiritual realm, they appear in Ephesians as "...*loins girt about with truth, and having on the breastplate of righteousness; And your feet shod with the preparation of the gospel of peace; Above all, taking the shield of faith, wherewith ye shall be able to quench all the fiery darts of the wicked. And take the helmet of salvation, and the sword of the Spirit, which is the Word of GOD: Praying always with all prayer*

---

[57] Proverbs 10:22

[58] Mark 9:29

Chapter 6: Check-in Or Carry-on

and supplication in the Spirit, and watching thereunto with all perseverance and supplication for all saints...[59]"

They are produced by living and walking in the spirit. Continous praying and fasting are essential weapons in our ongoing warfare; along with truth, righteousness, peace, faith, salvation, and the Word of GOD[60].

So we are told here our Carry-on Luggage must include: the whole armor of GOD which will include our Holy Bible and scriptures engraved on our hearts. A good pilot learns to wake up each morning with their Carry-on luggage ready for travel. They have long since realized that GOD promises new loads of blessing[61] each morning and they are prepared to use them.

We must be like the woman with the issue of blood[62], not afraid to press toward the mark to receive our treasure. She left behind all of what society thought about her in order to become free. She was not concerned about packing unnecessary baggage; she had to get to JESUS. She was singularly focused on her Carry-on Luggage.

I believe this woman, by her actions, had the essential weapons for warfare with her: truth, righteousness, peace, faith, salvation and the Word of GOD. She received and acted on her personal Word from GOD. She had made a choice to get to JESUS and that choice freed her of all her luggage, making her whole.

The journey from trash to treasure is the journey to wholeness; not just recovery in a certain aspect of your life, but to truly be moving towards all GOD has called you to be. The first stage of our actual journey (the packing) must begin with leaving and then cleaving to the promise GOD has for us, all HIS treasure.

---

[59] Ephesians 6:14-18

[60] Galatians 5:25

[61] Psalms 68:19

[62] Matthew 9:19-21; Mark 5:24-28

Fly With GOD

The book of Deuteronomy references several times how we must cleave to the LORD. For many of us, this leaving and cleaving to the LORD has never actually taken place. We are still attached to people, places, thoughts and things. Until we are able to make the transition, we will be grounded "not able to Fly."

Remember, baggage is anything you are trying to bring on the plane despite its value; trash or luggage (treasure).[63] This chapter encourages you to bring with you only the treasured items. Items which increase in value as you move toward your destination.

I believe there are millions of people on Earth running to catch a plane, just like I did. But the only way to catch the plane GOD has for us is to travel with only our treasure. This requires that the baggage be of quality not quantity. The people, places, things, actions and thoughts must be of extreme value to take the journey; the *"Awesome Truth"* is they cannot be just OK.

Finally, our journey is long, so just like a marathon racer would never invest in marginal or just adequate sneakers; we must invest in the best also. Our relationships, memories and things must be the best for us.

So here are my questions to you: Will you surrender all of your baggage to the LORD? Will you let JESUS determine what's in your Carry-on Luggage? Will you leave procrastination? Will you divorce its heirs? Will you face today choosing to throw away any items which do not help you press toward the mark for the prize?

We all tell stories, but our story will remain a myth if we allow the "Awful Truth" of our lives to remain unchallenged by GOD's "Awesome Truth."

---

[63] Matthew 6:19-21

Chapter 6: Check-in Or Carry-on

Dear FATHER GOD,

YOU have revealed an awesome truth.
A truth I need hidden in my heart.
LORD, help me to dispel every myth that is contrary
to YOUR Word
Let me walk daily in YOUR living truth, focusing on YOU
and YOU only!

In JESUS Name – Amen

Meditation Scriptures

- *Philippians 4:8 (KJV) Finally, brethren, whatsoever things are true, whatsoever things are honest, whatsoever things are just, whatsoever things are pure, whatsoever things are lovely, whatsoever things are of good report; if there be any virtue, and if there be any praise, think on these things.*

Fly With GOD

Now that you have read this chapter, what areas have changed in your truth as it relates to people, places and things? What has GOD revealed to you during this time?

Your Truth Time	
Awful Truth	**Awesome Truth**
People	People
Place	Place
Things	Things

Completion Date: ___/___/___ - 2nd Time

Part 3:
Baggage Processing

Simplicity is making the journey of this life with just baggage enough.

— Charles Dudley Warner

Chapter 7: Defining Baggage Processing

DEFINING BAGGAGE PROCESSING: determining the level of scrutiny our baggage will have to undergo.

In the previous chapter, we analyzed our current baggage and started thinking about how to pack better. In this chapter, we will concentrate on how our current and future behavior determines how quickly our baggage passes through inspection. We will focus on the "Baggage Processing" continuum and the godly steps we have, will or can choose to take. I call it a continuum because it is a daily process which never stops. How these steps lead toward a contraband-free lifestyle. The subsequent pages reveal several common types of contraband and provide instructions on how to get rid of it.

Baggage processing gives us an opportunity to identify and eliminate all the contraband in our lives. This is not an easy task, that is, why we need to pay particular attention to the word "PROCESSING." The dictionary defines the word "PROCESSING" as a series of actions, changes or functions bringing about a result. It is not one action but often a series of actions needed to eliminate the contraband. Baggage processing, if done continuously, allows our bags to be put through GOD's prescribed standards and

Fly With GOD

procedures; inspecting them for contraband before we take them on our Spiritual Flight.

So What Is Contraband? Any item that stops, slows down, or artificially speeds up our journey is considered contraband. They are actions, behaviors, habits, and incidents that do not line up with the truth of JESUS CHRIST[64] on your flight. It is any person, place, or thing that is not GOD's best for us. It may appear as fear, slothfulness, complaining, disbelief, denial, greed, jealousy, hate, envy, anger, rebellion, unforgiveness, or so many other works of the flesh[65].

For the adults who left with Moses for the "Promised Land," the contraband was their complaining – it slowed them down, and finally it was either their rebellion[66] or disbelief[67] which stopped all but two (2) of them from entering the "Promised Land". In this case, contraband cost millions their Flight with GOD. For Abraham, it was fathering Ishmael[68] – which artificially sped up his journey. Because, he did not wait on GOD to bless Sarah with Isaac[69], Abraham's actions resulted in conflicts which continue to this day.

GOD looks at our actions. Whether it was Moses or Abraham "the father of many nations", GOD requires actions which line-up with HIS words. When actions don't line-up, they are contraband. If not properly processed, contraband separates us from GOD's promised journey for our lives. A thorough baggage inspection is necessary for us to process our baggage. We must effectively and continuously answer the following questions and act on the results we obtain.

---

[64] John 1:17

[65] Galatians 5:19-21

[66] Numbers 14:9-30 Children's rebellion

[67] Numbers 20:7-12 Moses and Aaron's disbelief

[68] Genesis 16:2-5

[69] Genesis 21:2

Chapter 7: Defining Baggage Processing

WHAT–WHY–WHEN–HOW
What Is The Contraband In Your Life?
Why Is This Type Of Contraband In Your Life?
When Should You Eliminate This Contraband From Your Life?
How Can You Eliminate This Contraband From Your Life?

The right answers and actions will allow us to continuously process our baggage in a godly fashion. The "Baggage Processing" requires us to not only rigorously screen for contraband, by answering the What and Why—but employ mechanisms for their timely demise, by answering the When and How.

WHAT Is The Contraband In Your Life? Contraband are thoughts and/or actions that have not lined up with the Word of GOD in our life. Often the assessment begins with a surface view of what WE believe is wrong with our life – thoughts, behaviors, habits, actions, and incidents. This initial screening looks at what GOD talks about when HE declares, HE will meet our needs. This screening deals with our initial "Awful Truth" the ungodly items we have in our baggage.

As we continue on our journey, we will come to realize that this assessment must go deeper to a geospatial level, which is, finding things above, on or below the surface. Each of us has our own thorns[70] in the flesh, some so obvious the world has taken great joy to identify, others hidden so deep we will only discover and/or uncover them with the LORD's continuous assistance along life's journey.

To better understand the importance of the "WHAT question," here is a biblical example of the children of Israel's journey from bondage to the desert, and then to the "Promised Land". The processing begins with their cry to come out of the Egyptian oppression. GOD meets their needs by sending Moses to deliver them out of bondage. GOD has a flight plan for them, a big plan. HE wants

---
[70] 2 Corinthians 12:7

Fly With GOD

to get rid of more of the WHATs in their lives; behaviors, habits and actions!

As the baggage processing continues, we see GOD's plan was for them to go from bondage to bountifulness, but along the way they find out there are a lot of WHATs separating them from their destination. The processing used to get them to the "Promised Land" took over 40 years to finish. A lot of the contraband that was brought into the desert by the Hebrews had to be left behind before they could cross into the "Promised Land".

Some of the WHATs were things like fear, doubting, murmuring, complaining, jealousy, grumbling, quarrelling, and refusing to follow instructions. This contraband had to be left in the desert, before they were able to Fly. So for these Hebrew children, crossing the Red Sea represented the beginning of their "Awful Truth" in leaving their contraband behind in order to provide an inheritance for their children and their children's children in the Promise Land.

WHY Is This Type Of Contraband In Your Life? The effects of our thoughts, behaviors, habits, actions, and incidents play a vital role in determining the kind of contraband we have in our life. We all have thorns in our flesh, they maybe similar, but they are not exactly the same. Your experiences, both good and bad, have a major impact on the types of contraband that exist and their power on your life.

When Elijah told the woman from Zaraphath to "Fear Not" and to use the last of the meal to feed him first, that fear was contraband[71]. Why was this type of fear in this woman's life? The facts revealed that the severe drought had dried up the food supply. People around her were dying of starvation. Many of us will find the answer to our WHY – is also some supply we had counted on has or is about to dry up.

---

[71] 1 King 17: 13

Chapter 7: Defining Baggage Processing

WHEN Should You Eliminate This Contraband From Your Life? In GOD's proper time for you!

It is written "To every thing there is a season, and a time to every purpose under the heaven."[72] If you are listening to the LORD, HE is faithful to nudge you when it is time to eliminate a particular contraband. This journey would be impossible if you had to wake up one morning and be contraband free. Instead, GOD gives you revelation during your journey which allows you to eliminate the contraband at the appropriate time.

Consider something as common as a callus or corn on your foot. You may continue for weeks—if not years without the need for medical attention. Then suddenly the corn or callus becomes so uncomfortable you can hardly walk. What do you do? You seek medical attention to eliminate it. At this point, you are ready to eliminate this item from your life. The pain was your nudge—the season is now.

King David was called a man after GOD's heart. But he was also a man with a lot of contraband. His journey before and after he became king is filled with stories of how he eliminated his contraband when GOD nudged. I believe he was called a man after GOD's heart because of what he did when GOD called him to eliminate contraband. King David was quick to listen – quick to respond – and even quicker to act on GOD's Word.

HOW Can You Eliminate This Contraband From Your Life? This question is most definitely the hardest to answer and act on. It requires us to move from the assessment to the implementation process where we deal with our "Awesome Truth." The truth that you are able to change your mind, body and soul to desire and act on whatever is true[73] by using GOD's two-edged sword[74]

---

[72] Ecclesiastes 3:1

[73] Philippians 4:8

[74] Hebrews 4:12

Fly With GOD

of revelation and knowledge. This is accomplished by sowing, scraping, and sharpening your mind, body and soul.

GOD has sowed into each of us a Word from HIM that is as unique as your fingerprints. That Word is the standard your contraband must be assessed against. If an item in your baggage meets the minimum standard, it has to be sharpened – making it better. If an item fails to meet the standard it must be scraped away.

Scraping away eliminates the initial contraband, sowing fills the empty spaces so no new contraband can take root there, while sharpen refines. The scraping and sharpening are used to ensure flight preparedness by getting rid of contraband; loosening the roots of embedded contraband. These processes together allow you to gain speed, lift and sustainability.

Sowing GOD's truth ensures that you don't replace one type of contraband with another. The Book of Matthew and Luke both warn against the dangers of casting out one form of contraband to have it later replaced with seven (7) other more deadly than the first contraband[75].

Gastric bypass surgery is a modern day example of the challenges of a patient not properly sowing. Doctors all over the world have documented how food addictions are being replaced with even deadlier addictions: drugs, alcohol, sex and others. The psychiatric industry is warning individuals that they must deal with the root of their contraband, otherwise they will be possibly trading one addiction for many more, what they call "addiction transfer."

Since contraband may often be habits we have engaged in for a long-time, they may be rooted deep within us. The roots of these behaviors can become grafted in. The process of scraping may still leave the roots of the contraband. In these cases sowing of GOD's Word-in-action will be critical to their separation and uprooting.

---

[75] Matthew 12:43-45, Luke 11:24-26

Chapter 7: Defining Baggage Processing

As Ephesians 6 states, we will need to have on the full "Armor of GOD" to eliminate contraband. The roots can be much stronger than we can ever imagine, so we must be fully armed and ready. We will need ALL the spiritual weapons to eradicate contraband. Our weapons: truth, righteousness, peace, faith, and salvation. These weapons must be active to uproot contraband.[76]

Only when enough Word-in-action has been planted into our spirit will we have the power necessary to scrape out that contraband at the root and replace it with the treasure discussed in the previous chapter. Our successful *"baggage processing"* is based on our ability to persistently apply a series of godly actions to our own baggage which will eradicate contraband and reveal the priceless treasure GOD has for us.

In the next few chapters, I will reveal the most highly explosive types of contraband: fear, disbelief, unforgiveness, slothfulness, and rebellion. These items are the easiest to slip into believers' luggage. The consequences of not being on guard every moment will lead to baggage inspection failure. All it takes is a telephone call, a quick glance away or an overactive imagination and the contraband slips in. If we do not constantly screen our baggage, we are liable to try to bring these unauthorized materials on our flight.

Dear LORD,

In YOUR perfect timing, please grant each one of us the eyes to see, the ears to hear and most importantly the heart to eliminate any actions, behaviors, habits, and incidents that do not line up with the grace and truth of JESUS CHRIST – Amen

---

[76] Ephesians 6:13-18

Fly With GOD

Meditation Scriptures

- *Zechariah 13:9 (KJV)... through the fire, and will refine them as silver is refined, and will try them as gold is tried: they shall call on my name, and I will hear them: I will say, It is my people: and they shall say, The LORD is my GOD.*

The following is a list of common contraband, which items can you find in your luggage, today? (Place check marks by the items)

___Fear	___Jealousy
___Slothfulness	___Hate
___Complaining	___Envy
___Disbelief	___Anger
___Denial	___Rebellion
___Greed	___Unforgiveness

___Other:_____

Chapter 8: Contraband: Fear

FEAR: Worries, fright, dread, and anxiety that GOD will not keep HIS Word to you.

Is Fear Your Contraband? Fear of Flying whether in the natural or the spiritual is about our vulnerability and inability to surrender our life to another. Flying in the natural is one of the safest forms of transportation. The United States National Safety Council provides statistics that tell us that we are at least 22 times safer in a plane than an automobile[77]. But, yet I can't remember anyone telling me they were afraid of getting in an automobile, unless the driver was drinking or incompetent.

In the Bible, GOD has provided us statistics that support HIS 100% success rate. HE keeps HIS promises. But sadly enough, neither statistic has changed the minds of the millions of people each and every day who are afraid to Fly.

Fear is one of the most pervasive enemies of GOD's best. As contraband, fear is an unstable and highly volatile substance. Fear it is capable of penetrating every aspect of your journey to flight.

---

[77] Driving or Flying? Plane vs. Car Accident Statistics, http://www.Flyingfear.net/articles/how-safe-is-Flying-detailed-statistics.html, ,(Posted on 05:57, July 1st, 2009)

Fly With GOD

This enemy is notorious for spreading rumors throughout every part of your life.

Fear loves to pretend to be your friend. Fear will whisper in your ear to be very careful, you might get hurt. Fear will fill your head with worries, fright, and anxiety. It will make you think right is wrong; and wrong is right, and urge you to act on that misinformation. Fear likes using earthly facts and fiction to shake your godly peace and courage.

For instance, when Pharaoh pursued the children of Israel, they feared drowning in the Red Sea. Earthly facts revealed they had two choices, go back and be captured or move forward and drown. By trusting these earthly facts, they became fearful. As a result of their fear, they said, they would rather have stayed in Egypt as slaves to their cruel masters, than to die free in the wilderness. They actually believed that GOD would allow Pharaoh's army to capture them or the Red Sea to drown them.

The miracles the children of Israel had personally witnessed did not increase their peace and courage. They were wrong; their fears were unfounded. GOD not only provided a dry path in the middle of the Red Sea for them but allowed that same path to drown their enemies. Same path different results. The difference is who sent them.

What Type of Fear? Fear-of-falling from the sky; it stops many Christians from actually Flying. They are afraid of missing the mark; being exposed; what people might say; and much more. These individuals fall into two categories: "Fair Mode" and "Good Mode". Neither category is aware of GOD's "Awesome Truth." Each mode believes that staying under the radar is more important than being completely obedient to what GOD calls them to do.

The individuals that live in what I call the "Fair Mode" have somehow convinced themselves that being "Fair" is what GOD wants and desires for them. Similar to the children of Israel, their

Chapter 8: Contraband: Fear

focus is on staying alive, in bondage, is more important than being free in the wilderness with GOD. They don't seem to grasp that GOD will lead them every step of the way in the wilderness.

These believers have chosen to crawl or walk in less than their godly inheritance. They believe if they stumble, they won't get-up. When believers don't understand the "Presence" of GOD – Jehovah Shammah or the Peace of GOD – Jehovah Shalom, they live in fear. For them living righteously means making sure that their personal safety net has been properly erected. Personal safety nets which insure minimal damage while providing a level of comfort. The idea of reaching further immediately brings feelings of fear. These individuals have erroneously confused comfort with GOD's calling, so they stay on the ground. These individuals have thus made a personal decision to be grounded.

Individuals living in the "Good Mode" are not much better, possibly worse. They are victims of the insidious nature of fear. Fear's stealth nature can make them believe, they are peaceful and living in GOD's presence, but it is nothing more than a shade of fear. Generally, these individuals have seen more of GOD's supernatural power in their life, than most. They have experience blessings and miracles first hand, but they still pull back from living in GOD's total presence.

Even the disciples which walked with JESUS were sometimes infected with fear. In Mark 4, the disciples are in the boat with JESUS when the waves begin to fill it. They are so frighten of dying, they wake HIM up. JESUS rebukes the wind and says to the sea, "Peace Be Still", and the sea becomes calm. What makes fear so insidious is that even when JESUS was there in the boat, HIS physical presence is still not enough to dispel the disciples' fear of perishing. Only when JESUS calms the sea, are their fears relieved.

There are two (2) important facts in this passage: the first, JESUS' presence and the second, a raging storm. In order for fear to triumph,

Fly With GOD

the disciples had to disregard the power of JESUS's spiritual presence even as HE slept near them and pay attention to the storm.

The disciples accepted JESUS' physical presence but not HIS spiritual presence. They did not understand that both were there. Instead the disciples acted on an incomplete truth – paying attention to the storm rather than the presence of JESUS. An incomplete truth occurs in "Flying" when you fail to take into account all of the facts. The fact that the power of the LORD in any situation rules!

Much like the disciples what we choose to pay attention to – determines whether we operate in fear or peace. No additional element is ever needed when we have GOD on our side. Remember how one angel of the LORD came out of the spiritual realm into the natural realm to kill 185,000 Assyrians in just one night on behalf of Jerusalem[78]. This is the complete truth you and I live in.

The accomplishments of individuals living in the "Good Mode" are often made up of a combination of self-works and GOD's unlimited mercy. These individuals work extremely hard at their occupation. They pencil GOD in, and when available keep the appointment. Their relationships with GOD are inconsistent and thus their accomplishments are temporal.

These individuals have distorted James 2:14 where it *says "What doth it profit, my brethren, though a man say he hath faith, and have not works? can faith save him?"* These people don't understand that James wanted them not to just learn all the right things to do and say, but to actually do something with that knowledge. He knew Christians needed both to succeed. If James were alive today, I believe he would say let me be clear "works" are the output from all of the godly actions accomplished to bring about a GOD–driven results.

---

[78] 2 Kings 19:34-35

Chapter 8: Contraband: Fear

They fear going after "GOD's BEST." Membership in the world's winners circle is enough for the "Good Mode" people. They know it will cost and they believe the risk is too great. The idea of Flying with GOD is for the other guy. They'd rather stay safely in the "Good Mode" than risk a public humiliation by crashing.

We can only conclude that their current successes without the faith component are a form of godliness. Their distortion of James' message is used to support strategies for even more earthly successes. These successes are the result of a dash of faith, little risk, and finally fear.

These underperformers say: Isn't running good enough? I'm a good Christian right? But the question back to them must be – Why are you on the ground instead of in the air? Is living in any fear, no matter how small, living GOD's Best?

How many opportunities to "Fly" have you missed because of similar circumstances?

Are you letting your works get in the way?

Are you letting your works get in the way?

How can you eliminate Fear? Through scraping and/or a sharpening process our fear which is built on false beliefs are replaced by truth. Somehow Christians in both "Modes" have a false belief that staying at a marginal or less than best place is a guarantee of peace, safety, and blessings. They don't understand that less-fear is very different from fear-less.

Fear draws its strength from your ignorance of all the blessings and curses stated in the Bible. It is impossible to remain fearful when you are immersed in the promises' of GOD and answering HIS call. When we read, *"From everyone who has been given much, much will be demanded; and from the one who has been entrusted with*

Fly With GOD

much, much more will be asked[79]." We realize an "Awesome Truth" <u>all</u> of our actions count.

The only thing we should fear is being called a "lazy servant" by the LORD; and not receiving all the jewels in our crown. What we do for GOD counts—all our actions count.

Fear is rooted in ignorance of GOD's Word for us. We become fearful when we are not sowing GOD's truth into our spirit. In Hosea[80] it states clearly that, *"My people are destroyed for lack of knowledge: because thou hast rejected knowledge, I will also reject thee..."*

Not knowing the truth about our past, present and future can cause us harm. The "Awesome Truth" is if we know that GOD sent us, then we must also know that we can't fail.

GOD writes, on every order "Mission Accomplished." Our master provides the plane, flight-plan, fuel, supplies, and HIS winning strategy. Our new knowledge must be an understanding that GOD equips us for our predestinated[81] journey. HE prepares and sustains our flight.

Be not afraid,[82] remember what the LORD did to Pharaoh. Here GOD reminds us of HIS miracle—working power. Fear in the obedient believer is unfounded[83]. HIS Word clearly tells us we will have battles and HE is with us. HE is great and the only one to be feared. Thus, every failed attempt either scrapes out contraband or sharpens us. GOD does all of this to bring us closer to the truth that we were born to fly.

---

[79] Luke 12:48 (NIV)

[80] Hosea 4:6 (KJV)

[81] Rom 8:29-30; Eph 1:5-11

[82] Deuteronomy 7:18

[83] Only fear of GOD—Ecclesiastes 12:13; 1 Peter 2:17; and Revelation 14:7

Chapter 8: Contraband: Fear

How many times did Thomas Edison fail trying to create a durable light bulb before success was achieved? If your answer was over 1,000 times[84], you're right, and that wasn't his greatest invention. He knew a secret that so few of us are able to grasp and thus he was not afraid. That is, what seems like failure is often GOD's way of scraping and sharpening—bringing us one step closer to an even greater success.

Eliminating fear can only happen if we assess our shortcoming and failures much like Mr. Edison did time and time again. We can take this new knowledge, and try again, and again and again, until we "Fly." So is this assess and try again process biblical? Yes!

The Old Testament gives us Proverbs 24:16 which says, *"...a just man falleth seven times, and riseth up again: but the wicked shall fall into mischief."* The New Testament gives us the Apostle Peter, a man in CHRIST's inner circle as a living example of fear in action. Peter, having personally witnessed thousands of miracles, still denied JESUS CHRIST three (3) times. Later, we see that Peter assessed his failures, tried again and courageously preached the Gospel. How did he do that? by accepting and acting on GOD's Word that he could fly.

So now you know it is not the crash that matters, it is your ability to focus on the truth by getting back up and flying. When you are able to identify your fears you uncovered an "Awful Truth." You counter it by sowing into your spirit, scriptures supporting the Presence of GOD which is Jehovah—Shammah and Peace of GOD which is Jehovah—Shalom.

The GOD that is always here – giving you peace. GOD is here, calming your fears and allowing you to see the "Awesome Truth". The truth of who you are. The truth of what you have been called

---

[84] National Park Service, US Department of the Interior, www.nps.gov/archive/edis/edifun/edifun_4andup/timeline.htm, Thomas Edison timeline.

Fly With GOD

to do. The truth of the protection which will always be in and around you.

You are not covering up contraband. You are scraping it out. The hole that is left by fear's exit – is now being replaced with the presence and peace of knowing you will succeed, "fear not[85]."

What you have been called to do can be stormy. You can be fasting, praying and still be in the storm. Fear can grip you to the point that you wonder if the LORD realizes you are out there doing HIS will. I have good news for you. The LORD is in the storm with you, HE loves hanging out with HIS disciples. How can I be sure? Because the Bible says even in the midst of HIS disciples' divine journey, a storm arose and HE was present.

> *The passage states: "… HE (JESUS) was in the hinder part of the ship, asleep on a pillow: and they (the disciples) awake HIM, and say unto HIM, MASTER, carest thou not that we perish? And HE arose, and rebuked the wind, and said unto the sea, Peace, be still. And the wind ceased, and there was a great calm. And HE said unto them, Why are ye so fearful?[86]"*

What is important is that ANY journey JESUS sends you on, the HOLY SPIRIT will be there. There is no need to wake HIM, HE never sleeps.[87] HE provides you blessed assurances of this truth in HIS Word. Fear may have affected the beginning of the story for the disciples in the boat, but it didn't end there, because GOD was there. The truth for this story and yours is just because GOD is not responding the way you want HIM to – does not mean you should be afraid or turn back. HE cares for HIS beloved and is always there.

---

[85] Deuteronomy 1:21, 20:3, 31:6

[86] Mark 4:38-40

[87] Psalms 121:4

Chapter 8: Contraband: Fear

A sky with clouds may actually be what your spirit is longing for. In Exodus, the LORD sends the clouds[88] to the children of Israel in the desert to guide them daily to the Promised Land. As we get stronger in the LORD, we are able to be content with whatever state we are in whether in a cloud, valley or on the mountain top. We are sharpened by GOD's promises to give strength[89] to HIS people and bless them with peace. The peace, we produced when we love GOD's law[90] and do not become [91]afraid no matter how many clouds appear.

Fear is something that we overcome with JESUS. On the subsequent pages you should list some of your fears. Fears are like footprints, they are similar but never the same. They are unique to our personal experiences and easily brushed away with the help of JESUS. No one has fears quite like yours.

The "Awesome Truth" is that JESUS can cast out all fears; even your peculiar ones. HIS promises can and will provide the peace needed to calm any fears. The more you are able to sow the "Word of GOD" in your life the more you will be able to conquer any fears that separate you from Flying High.

Dear LORD,

Please give me the strength to live bravely, courageously, and fearless for YOU – GOD. In the midst of any struggles allow me to experience YOUR peace, transforming any fears into godly expectations. AMEN

---

[88] Exodus 13:21

[89] Psalm 29:11

[90] Psalm 119:165

[91] John 14:27

Meditation Scriptures

- *Luke 12:7 (KJV) But even the very hairs of your head are all numbered. Fear not therefore: ye are of more value than many sparrows.*

- *Romans 8:15 (KJV) For ye have not received the spirit of bondage again to fear; but ye have received the Spirit of adoption, whereby we cry, Abba, FATHER.*

- *2 Timothy 1:7 (KJV) For GOD hath not given us the spirit of fear; but of power, and of love, and of a sound mind.*

- *Hebrews 13:6 (KJV) So that we may boldly say, The LORD is my helper, and I will not fear what man shall do unto me.*

- *1 John 4:18 (KJV) There is no fear in love; but perfect love casteth out fear: because fear hath torment. He that feareth is not made perfect in love.*

- *John 16:33 (KJV) These things I have spoken unto you, that in me ye might have peace. In the world ye shall have tribulation: but be of good cheer; I have overcome the world.*

Chapter 8: Contraband: Fear

Fear can stop you from Flying with GOD if you let it. Throughout the Bible we find individuals who either overcame their fears and flew with GOD or stayed in fear and failed to Fly.

What fears are you experiencing today? In the chart below, list each and every one of those fears in the 1st column; no matter what the size and cause. Here comes the hard part, in the 2nd column list what GOD has revealed to you during your time of meditation. Indicate the ways you can experience GOD's peace when the fears appear in your life.

Your Truth Time	
Awful: Fears	**Awesome: Peace**
1.	1.
2.	2.
3.	3.
4.	4.
5.	5.
6.	6.
7.	7.

Completion Date: ___/___/___

Chapter 9:
Contraband: Disbelief

DISBELIEF – Reluctance to believe ALL of GOD's promises to you.

Is disbelief your contraband? Some Christians go through the motions of believing. It is what I call the ministry of "fake-it until you make-it", which really is plain old fashioned disbelief. They just don't trust GOD to do all HE said HE would. They have learned to pray as a matter of fact, not ever expecting miracles from the LORD. What once was a childhood promise has now become their modern day myth. They don't understand that it is impossible[92] to please GOD without faith.

What happens to all those Christians living the myth? These Christians never make-it. Faking-it never leads to flight.

What type of Disbelief? The contraband of disbelief is the hardest to identify in a Christian. This contraband always exists with a measure of faith. They have faith, when they confess that JESUS CHRIST is LORD, and believe GOD raised HIM from the dead. This may be the only measure of faith they have. But the faith to believe that GOD will meet all their needs is missing.

---

[92] Hebrews 11:6

Chapter 9: Contraband: Disbelief

Faith and disbelief can occupy our thoughts simultaneously. We can believe strongly in the death to eternal life aspect of Christianity, but fail to understand the born again to living on earth aspect. We are able to believe that JESUS died and was resurrected, that if we follow JESUS when we die, we will be resurrected. This powerful dying faith walks hand-in-hand with the weak living faith.

JESUS talks about living faith when HE says, " ...Verily I say unto you, If ye have faith, and doubt not, ye shall not only do this which is done to the fig tree, but also if ye shall say unto this mountain, Be thou removed, and be thou cast into the sea; it shall be done[93]." So the challenge for many Christians is not their dying faith, but how to increase their living faith to eliminate disbelief.

How can you eliminate disbelief? The "Awful Truth" for many Christians is that they operate daily in a measure of disbelief. Their inability or refusal to believe or to accept what GOD has whispered to them hampers them from Flying. This unbelief causes millions of mountains not to be moved for the Kingdom.

If these Christians only knew the "Awesome Truth" of how important it is to expect a miracle, they would immediately start sowing earnest prayers for increased faith. They would ask JESUS to work on their faith, much like the father who had a demon possessed son in the Book of Mark. His earnest belief and godly anticipation, is what JESUS loves.

> *JESUS said to him, "if thou canst believe, all things are possible to him that believeth. And straightway the father of the child cried out, and said with tears, LORD, I believe; help thou mine unbelief"*[94].

This man's measure of disbelief was changed to faith with his earnest prayers. Here we had a father who wanted to believe so

---

[93] Matthew 21:21

[94] Mark 9:23-24 (KJV)

Fly With GOD

desperately, but realizing that if he doesn't have the right level of belief, his son will not be healed. So he immediately takes out a spiritual insurance policy to be guaranteed by JESUS CHRIST. He says to JESUS, if I'm lacking in the necessary faith, stand in the gap and strengthen my belief. This father understood how faith and disbelief could be operating together and he wanted only faith.

The King James Version of this passage I like best because it said the father cried out. I can actually see the tears of a parent that has suffered year after year in turmoil over their child's condition. This father was asking JESUS to instantly replace his wavering faith with steadfast immovable faith. This father knew the "Awesome Truth" the secret of getting what you need.

The secret is to ask the GIVER! He realized that any amount of disbelief would not do. This man needed mountain-moving belief. He got it! At that moment GOD scraped out any disbelief in the supernatural and replaced it with life-saving faith. The faith which creates miracles.

As believers, we must remind ourselves that JESUS is waiting for us to ask those four (4) simple words: *"LORD HELP MY UNBELIEF"*. Can't you hear the keys clanging? I can! That's the sound of the gates being opened wide and you being led into HIS presence.

Do you really need to be as desperate as that father was in the Book of Mark to finally ask JESUS for help? Are you so willful, prideful and/or stubborn; or to the contrary are you so naïve that you fail to ask? Whatever the reason, disobedience or ignorance, isn't it time to become truly "Faith-Based Christians" in both your dying and living faith?

The "Awful Truth" if not eliminated has consequences. Here is some important historical information about the dangers of disbelief from the book of Exodus, Chronicles and Samuel.

Chapter 9: Contraband: Disbelief

When the children of Israel journeyed from Egypt to the Promised Land, they showed their lack of faith in numerous situations. They refused to believe Caleb and Joshua's report, resulting in a 40 year journey instead of a couple of weeks. They chose to cry, complain and finally plot to replace Moses in order to return to Egypt, resulting in more punishment.

GOD showed the children of Israel miraculous wonders both in Egypt and the wilderness. This did not matter; they still treated GOD with contempt. GOD's final response after showing so much mercy was to allow them to wander in the wilderness until the disbelieving adults perished. The "Awful Truth" is that disbelief can lead to death, bondage or staying in the wilderness, if you do not replace it with faith.

King David[95] reminds us of how self-importance can affect our faith even when we have a strong relationship with GOD. It can make us believe but in the wrong thing—us. Here we find David having won hundreds of battles for the LORD. He is starting to feel a bit cocky. He has gone from having a vagabond army to a top-notch one. King David must have gotten very comfortable because we are told that Satan was able to cause him to take a census of the number of fighting men in Israel. When one of his confidants tells him of the danger of such an action; he even overrules him.

GOD's response to King David's actions was to send a plague causing 70,000 men of Israel to die in less than 72 hours. The "Awesome Truth" was that once David repented and let his actions support his belief in GOD, the plague stopped.

How do we stop the contraband of disbelief from getting in or taking over our luggage? We stop it when we recognize that disbelief is a leech sucking our faith dry – causing weak dreams, visions and hopes. By engaging in a spiritual scraping and sowing process, disbelief is eradicated and replaced it with faith.

---

[95] 1 Chronicles 21

Fly With GOD

> It is this belief in a power larger than myself and other than myself which allows me to venture into the unknown and even the unknowable.
>
> Maya Angelou

King David at Ziklag[96] is a great example of how not to let disbelief get comfortable in your luggage. When he felt distressed by his city burning, and the families taken captive; David chose to encouraged himself in the LORD. He prayed asking GOD for guidance and followed instructions. Once David received the Word from the LORD, he was faithful—unmoved by how bad the circumstances seemed, or what the people were saying around him. He went as GOD directed and recovered <u>all</u> that had been taken from Ziklag.

Have you ever had an experience like King David did at Ziklag? You know what I'm talking about, one where you have unbelievable success at work only to come home and face utter disaster. Or maybe your Ziklag experience was exactly like King David's – where you come home to a house on fire and your family is gone. Your relatives and friends not only blamed you, but are discussing your demise. If so, did you handle it like King David?

Ziklag is reminder that you can be doing the work of the LORD and bad things can still happen. But just like David you can overcome it with the LORD's help. We should not let fear stop us from Flying higher no matter how much is on fire. We need to stay in touch with the MASTER and follow HIS commands.

Disbelief stops or slows down flight. You need the Word to reverse the effects of this unhealthy condition. A daily regimen of hearing from GOD scrapes away disbelief and sharpens your faith. The "Word-of" and "the-Word-from" GOD will always eradicate disbelief and develop your faith.

---

[96] 1 Samuel 30

Chapter 9: Contraband: Disbelief

Faith is built-up by a daily regimen of devotion, hearing, reading, praying, and praising the LORD. When we take in more Word – it produces more faith allowing us to effectively and efficiently cast out disbelief. GOD increases our understanding, strength and skill.

The higher we Fly, the more time we must spend strengthening our faith. Let's look at two (2) passages from the Book of Romans that support this process. *"So then faith cometh by hearing, and hearing by the Word of GOD[97]"* and *"he that doubteth is damned if he eat, because he eateth not of faith: for whatsoever is not of faith is sin[98]."*

Finally, in the Book of Luke[99] a centurion displays great faith in JESUS. He tells JESUS, "I don't need you to come, but just speak the healing word and I know it will be done." JESUS' response, "I have not found so great faith, no, not in Israel." Can HE say that about you? If not, you need to build your faith even more. The Book of James describes it best by stating, faith without works is dead[100]; you have to work to build your faith up. Here, James reminds the believer that if your faith is increasing, so is your altitude.

Dear LORD,

I believe YOUR report for every situation I face.
My actions reflect the report YOU have given me
For I "FLY" by faith, not by sight[101].

Thank you In JESUS Name

---

[97] Romans 10:17

[98] Romans 14:23

[99] Luke 7:1-10

[100] James 2:20

[101] 2 Cor 5:7 Adapted

Fly With GOD

Meditation Scriptures

- *Romans 3:21-23 (NIV) But now a righteousness from GOD, apart from law, has been made known, to which the Law and the Prophets testify. This righteousness from GOD comes through faith in JESUS CHRIST to all who believe ...*

- *Galatians 3:6-8 (NIV) Consider Abraham: "He believed GOD, and it was credited to him as righteousness." Understand, then, that those who believe are children of Abraham. The Scripture foresaw that GOD would justify the Gentiles by faith, and announced the gospel in advance to Abraham: "All nations will be blessed through you."*

What areas are you weak in faith, where are you strong?

Your Truth Time	
Awful: Disbelief	**Awesome: Faith**
1.	1.
2.	2.
3.	3.
4.	4.
5.	5.

Completion Date: ___/ ___/ ___

Chapter 10: Contraband: Unforgiveness

UNFORGIVENESS: Reluctance or refusal to forgive an individual of a real or perceived harm.

Is Unforgiveness your contraband? GOD looks at unforgiveness the same as any other contraband: as a separation from the LORD GOD. To be unforgiving is the unwillingness to show mercy for a wrong. Unforgiveness separates us from GOD, whether it is because we have not forgiven others or ourselves.

In Chapter 2 of this book, I first introduced forgetting and forgiving as critical elements to Spiritual Flight [102]. There I discussed how when these elements are left undone they create contraband in your baggage. In the LORD's Prayer JESUS said, "For if ye forgive men their trespasses, your heavenly FATHER will also forgive you: But if ye forgive not men their trespasses, neither will your FATHER forgive your trespasses [103]." HE wanted you and I to understand how unforgiving leads to a life without peace and joy, but more importantly separation from HIM.

The New Testament is filled with passages which tell the story of this contraband. How our SAVIOR forgives and the dangers of

---

[102] Forgetting and Forgiving

[103] Matthew 6:14-15

Fly With GOD

unforgiveness. While JESUS was on the cross, HE said, "Forgive them for they know not what they do[104]." HE was forgiving HIS executioners while they still believed they were doing the right thing. They, much like us at times were unaware of their need for forgiveness. The Bible says, we have all done something wrong (sinned).[105] JESUS died and rose again so we could choose[106] CHRIST and not only be saved, but forgiven for those sins.

What type of Unforgiveness? Unforgiveness is our inability to forgive someone we believe has caused us harm. This belief can be real or perceived. The harm can be accidental or intentional. The offending party can be self and/or others. The common thread is that we have consciously or subconsciously not forgiven them. These forms of unforgiveness are dangerous whether they are focused on others or self—the result of which separates us from the will of GOD.

The Bible is full of men and women operating in GOD's forgiveness. On the way to Damascus, GOD presents to us Saul[107] who realizes only after he is blinded by JESUS that he is in the wrong job. He is not supposed to be persecuting Christians for a living, but leading and supporting them. Saul is given a new name, Paul that supports his future not his past.

Paul's future is full of personal and godly forgiveness. He was there at Stephen's stoning. Paul must have heard Stephen ask GOD to forgive him[108]. You don't read anything about Paul living a life of condemnation, recrimination or self loathing. Instead, the Apostle Paul spends the remainder of his life sharing the forgiveness GOD gave him with others. Paul provides chapter after chapter of vivid

---

[104]Luke 23:34

[105]Romans 3:23

[106]Romans 5:8

[107]Acts 9

[108]Acts 7:60

Chapter 10: Contraband: Unforgiveness

accounts of GOD's unlimited mercy, grace and peace as he continued Flying.

And let's not forget King David, who GOD declared was a man after HIS own heart[109]. Remember how David forgave King Saul each time he tried to kill him. What about forgiving Nabal? Abigail's[110] foolish husband who refused to give David food after he helped him. David forgave him too.

Can you also remember when King David commits adultery[111] with Bathsheba? He conceives a child out of that adulterous relationship, and murders her husband (Uriah, a just man) to conceal their affair. Later, we find him counting his warriors[112] as if that is what is needed to win a battle. King David's adulthood displays more than one instance of GOD's forgiveness. David reminds us all that though the journey is full of stumbles and falls, <u>it is forgiveness that matters</u>.

Neither Paul nor David allowed the consequences of their sins to deter them from fully serving the LORD. They are examples of men who committed numerous documented sins; one man before he knew GOD and one after. Their paths to repentance are very different, but GOD's forgiving nature is always the same. HE forgives – and so did they. The contraband of unforgiveness was not in their luggage, they were able to Fly high.

How can you eliminate Unforgiveness? The love of GOD is clothed in compassion, kindness, humility, gentleness and patience[113]. Love which Apostle Paul refers to in Colossians, allows you to eliminate the elements of unforgiveness in your baggage such as

---

[109] 1 Samuel 13:14; Acts 13:22

[110] 1 Samuel 25

[111] 2 Samuel 11-12

[112] 2 Samuel 24

[113] Colossians 3:12-14

cruelty, harshness, hatred, meanness, mercilessness, arrogance, pretentiousness, impatience, pride, hardness, intolerance, anger, madness, violence, dislike, hate, and scorn.

By carrying the garments of love, compassion, kindness, humility, gentleness, and patience you are able to eliminate contraband of unforgiveness. These garments enable you to scrape out unforgiveness and sow in the treasures mentioned in Colossians. As you begin this process of replacing the contraband with GOD's luggage, you will be able to forgive as the LORD has forgiven you.

By <u>completely</u> forgiving the offending parties, you eliminate the contraband of unforgiveness. This kind of "forgiving"; is also found in the LORD's Prayer[114] JESUS says "...and forgive us our debts, as we forgive our debtors." We are instructed by GOD ALMIGHTY to ask for forgiveness of our own real or perceived, accidental or intentional offenses and to continue to forgive others or self for offenses. This passage also includes the benefits: the blessing of obedience (forgiving others) or the curses of disobedience (unforgiveness).

Unforgiveness of Others. Do you find yourself saying, "if I forgive them they are getting a free ride? It is not fair! What about their punishment? They haven't suffered enough!" Well, that is exactly what the prodigal son's brother was saying to his father in that parable[115].

Just like that wise father, GOD reminds you of an "Awesome Truth". You had and continue to have the blessings and favor of your FATHER. When you truly believe you are the apple of GOD's eye, you are less likely to be caught up in whether someone deserves your forgiveness. You are willing to forgive because you want

---

[114]Mathew 6

[115]Luke 15:28-32

Chapter 10: Contraband: Unforgiveness

to please your FATHER and you realize that vengeance is HIS[116] not yours.

I know you're thinking, "That's great, but I'm surely not JESUS or one of those disciples." You may have to honestly say you're more like the prodigal son's brother—you have limits to your ability to forgive. The Bible talks about wickedness in high places[117], so I know that the ways to inflict pain and suffering on ourselves and on others are limitless. What I also know to be true is that we have unlimited power to stop unforgiveness from festering in our lives. The answer, I believe lies in our design. We were created in HIS image. Thus, we have an untapped reservoir of forgiveness in us and the ability to use adversity just like JESUS did to triumph over evil.

Unforgiveness of Self. The most insidious contraband may be your inability to forgive yourself for accidental or intentional harm to you and/or others. Your inability to forgive can display itself in low self-esteem, guilt and leave footholds for addictive behaviors.

For many of us dealing with the truth about the role we played in these harmful acts can cause a tidal wave of revelations. To admit these acts along with their consequences may offer more challenges. When this occurs new questions often surface regarding blame, making it even more difficult to forgive yourself.

The sins and their after-effects may be affecting your life right now; negative consequences like having the wrong job, wrong spouse, unwanted pregnancy, a broken marriage, or even jail time. The outcome of your actions may be painful. GOD has not promised to always take you off the hook. HE has promised you—forgiveness.

Doubting Forgiveness. Christians can be stuck on whether they believe they have been forgiven of their past sins by the LORD,

---

[116]Romans 12:19

[117]Ephesians 6:12

Fly With GOD

others and finally themselves. They recognized their sin(s); sought JESUS' for forgiveness; and truly repented! If you are one of those believers; you still find yourself in a place of unforgiveness; a place where you are constantly being reminded of your past sins—then STOP IT right now. This is a trick of the enemy. You have been forgiven.[118]

If you're stuck in unforgiveness, I want you to understand that accepting forgiveness may be your hardest contraband challenge. Yes—I said hardest, because it is often shrouded in extreme secrecy, guilt, and shame. But the Bible tells you, that while you were yet a sinner CHRIST died[119] for you so that you could be made righteous (without sin).

If you have accepted JESUS then the rest of the Book of Romans must also be true which says there is no condemnation[120] for those who are in CHRIST JESUS and who follow HIS SPIRIT. It is time to scrape out those secrets, shame and guilt and sow in the righteousness of the LORD.

I'm sure you have heard of the 23rd Psalm. But have you paid attention to verse 3? Verse 3 says, "HE restoreth my soul: HE leadeth me in the paths of righteousness for HIS name's sake[121]." GOD is talking about you, right now. HE wants to scrape out unforgiveness if you let HIM, while sowing into you the ways that lead to HIS righteousness.

Isaiah 45:8 – Let the Skies Pour Down Righteousness

Forgiveness. The Apostle Paul was obedient in his forgiveness. He applied forgiveness wherever he journeyed and successfully

---

[118] Ephesians 11:7, 4:32; Colossians 1:14

[119] Romans 5:8

[120] Romans 8:1

[121] Psalm 23:3

Chapter 10: Contraband: Unforgiveness

stayed in the present; experiencing unspeakable joy[122]. Even when times seemed harsh on the outside, his declaration was that he could do all things through CHRIST[123]. His many prison experiences still did not make him bitter: he chose to forgive. He did not allow unforgiveness to become part of his life by letting anything separate him from GOD's perfect will.

Paul told the Corinthians to follow him as he followed CHRIST[124]. Paul lived a life knowing the LORD set his offenses as far as the East is from the West.[125] The GOD of the universe is not keeping count of your offenses. HE forgives you. You are required to do the same.

We know that GOD has held up HIS side of the promise to forgive. Can we say the same? Sadly, the answer is sometimes no. Lack of biblical knowledge and understanding in action has led to more and more unforgiveness. JESUS tells us, "What is forgiven by GOD needs to be forgiven by us and others." We can't force others to forgive us. But you and I can take control of our thoughts, forgive ourselves, and not give place to what others may say. We can get rid of those things that don't line up with what GOD has spoken to our hearts.

When the Bible speaks of "renewing of your mind" it provides you with detailed instructions on the things you should spend time thinking about. It tells you that you will be transformed by focusing your mind on those things that are "good," "acceptable," and the "perfect will of GOD."[126] It is your actions of love, compassion,

---

[122]Philippians 4:11-13

[123]Philippians 4:13

[124]1 Corinthians 11:1 emphasized

[125]Psalms 103:12

[126]Romans 12:2, And be not conformed to this world: but be ye transformed by the renewing of your mind, that ye may prove what is that good, and acceptable, and perfect, will of GOD.

Fly With GOD

kindness, humility, gentleness, and patience which sharpen your mind, body, and soul.

The New Testament tells us the Blood of JESUS redeems us[127] to forgive and be forgiven. It goes further in providing mankind with continuous instructions for complete forgiveness toward others. When Peter asked JESUS this question, "...how oft shall my brother sin against me, and I forgive him? till seven times? JESUS saith unto him, I say not unto thee, Until seven times: but, Until seventy times seven."[128] This message from JESUS was so you would forgive.

I believe JESUS knew the problems of this contraband. HE continued by explaining the dangers of unforgiveness to Peter using the Parable of the Unmerciful Servant[129]. In this story, a servant owed his master several million dollars. The master orders the servant, his family and property to be sold to pay off the unpaid debt. When the servant pleads for more time, the compassionate master cancels the servant's entire debt.

The servant upon receiving his master's forgiveness does something very different to his debtor. This servant finds a fellow servant that owes him less than twenty dollars. He badgers him for the money. When the servant begs for patience the unmerciful servant responds by throwing him in jail. When the master finds out what this unmerciful servant did, he responds by placing him in jail.

The message is consistent: forgive, forgive and forgive. All four Gospels[130] in the New Testament carry the message that you must forgive for without forgiving, you are told, you can't be forgiven. The last sentence of that parable is your reminder, "This is how

---

[127] 1 Peter 1:19

[128] Matthew 18:21-22

[129] Matthew 18:23-34

[130] Matthew 6:12,14-15; Matthew 18:21,35; Mark 11:26; Luke 6:37, 7:4, Luke 23:34

Chapter 10: Contraband: Unforgiveness

my heavenly FATHER will treat each of you unless you forgive your brother from your heart."[131]

The "Awful Truth" is that some of us have counted all the wrongs that have been perpetrated against us as if it were some sort of treasure. It is on our balance sheets as credits. Things which are owed to us by the offending parties: apologies, compensation, restitution, and much more. We have stored these wrongs up like great riches, ignorantly believing that they will increase in value with time.

Time to be real <u>honest</u>, are you like the man in chapter 10 of the Book of Mark[132]? You do not commit adultery, do not kill, do not steal, do not bear false witness, do not defraud, do not dishonor your father and mother. However, you have other hidden sins. The wrongs you keep padlocked in your mind as some sort of treasure. Let me tell you this, unforgiveness is not a treasure!

JESUS is now asking you to let go of what you treasure most, will you? Can you let go of your treasured wrongs? Can you consider the debt paid in full by JESUS? Can you accept a balance sheet with zeros in all the "wrongs" columns?

The "Awful Truth" is that GOD has told you about how wicked and deceitful[133] the heart of man can be; but the "Awesome Truth" is that HE has also told you, that only HE knows the truth. Knowing that GOD knows the truth provides you the power and strength to not allow the unforgiving hearts of people to stop you from experiencing GOD's best, which is to Fly.

Take up your cross and Fly with GOD!

---

[131]Matthew 18:35

[132]Mark 10:17-22

[133]Jeremiah 17:9

Dear LORD,

Help me every moment to follow YOU. I know when I follow YOU I leave a path of forgiveness wherever I go. Whether I am at home, work or at the marketplace my actions display mercy, grace, peace and love.

When I question a person's worthiness for forgiveness I remember what CHRIST did for me and that settles the issue.

My strength is in YOU – LORD.

I declare today – I WILL FORGIVE!

Thank you In JESUS Name

Meditation Scriptures

- Mark 11:25 (KJV) And when ye stand praying, forgive, if ye have ought against any: that your FATHER also which is in heaven may forgive you your trespasses.

- Luke 6:37 (KJV) Judge not, and ye shall not be judged: condemn not, and ye shall not be condemned: forgive, and ye shall be forgiven:

- Ephesians 4:32 (KJV) And be ye kind one to another, tenderhearted, forgiving one another, even as GOD for CHRIST's sake hath forgiven you.

Chapter 10: Contraband: Unforgiveness

It is time to trade in your counterfeit for real treasure. With much prayer, complete your list.

Your Truth Time: Unforgiveness	
Awful: Unforgiveness	**Awesome: Forgiveness**
1.	1.
2.	2.
3.	3.
4.	4.
5.	5.
6.	6.
7.	7.
8.	8.

Completion Date: ___/ ___/ ___

Chapter 11: Contraband: Slothfulness

SLOTHFULNESS: Doing the work GOD required you to do in a slow and/or lackadaisical pace.

The Parable of the Talents: Matthew 25:25-26 (The Message)

I was afraid I might disappoint you, so I found a good hiding place and secured your money. Here it is, safe and sound down to the last cent. The master was furious. That's a terrible way to live! It's criminal to live cautiously like that! If you knew I was after the best, why did you do less than the least?

Is Slothfulness your contraband? The above story is known as the "Parable of the Talents." I like the word talents because it best exposes the individual that chose to bury his giftedness from the world. Matthew tells the story of how each of us is given a different amount of talents. It is our job on earth to provide increase on what was given.[134] Not to return with the same amount we have been given.

Other versions of the Bible call the servant's behavior wicked, lazy, slothful, evil, and good-for-nothing. I do not want any of these

---
[134] Matthew 25

Chapter 11: Contraband: Slothfulness

words used to describe my use of talents when I get to Heaven. What about you? This story of the talents perfectly outlines the consequences of choosing to bury your gifts instead of Flying.

If you're a Christian you are most likely aware of the 10 commandments. You may even consider yourself a diligent follower of them. I would like to discuss an "Awful Truth," a sin that is often not talked about. Slothfulness—the sin which causes us to stay on the ground, rather than soar in the sky. In the book of Matthew[135], GOD calls this type of behavior wicked and slothful, when HE refers to the servant that buried his talents.

What type of Slothfulness? Slothfulness is why we might succumb to the practice of staying in a church where we feel our talents will remain safe. Hiding in the church and vain busyness are the most common areas of slothfulness for the sincere Christian. We may be great at sharing the Gospel with fellow believers, but spend little time, if any with unbelievers. We may be the hardest worker in your community, but if we are not working on the project GOD assigned, then we are slothful.

The "Parable of the Talents," reminds us how GOD determines if we have been slothful on earth, not people. Is the assignment HE gave you done? Did you work on it at all? The "Awful Truth" is the more work we leave undone, the more contraband we are carrying and the less likely we are to Fly high.

Hiding in the Church. The "Awesome Truth" is there is a *"Great Commission"* which JESUS spoke of in Matthew. "Go ye therefore, and teach all nations, baptizing them in the name of the FATHER, and of the SON, and of the HOLY GHOST."[136] The "Awful Truth" is that staying in the church and not going out into the world, is not of GOD. The LORD clearly reveals that HE is not pleased with this behavior. He has provided instruction on what HE desires. The Old

---

[135] Matthew 25

[136] Matthew 28:19 (KJV)

Fly With GOD

and New Testaments provide a blueprint for productiveness and preparedness. GOD calls us all through the valleys, then up to the mountains, and then finally in to the skies; all for HIS glory.

Remember the 23rd Psalm written by King David, The LORD is my shepherd. "Is" is not part of a question but a statement. I believe it is a declaration! It is recited so often you probably don't realize that right there GOD is calling you through the valley[137]. This valley is not an ordinary valley. David experienced this extraordinary valley, when he fought Goliath[138], sinned with Bathsheba[139], numbered his troops[140]; and much more. All of this I believe makes King David truly qualified to reveal the facts and truths about the valley experiences in this powerful Psalm.

The "Awful Truth" is that, death along with our enemies, linger in the valley. In the shadows their only job is to instill fear and steal our victories. We need to remember that a shadow cannot appear without light. The "Awesome Truth" is that light is GOD. HE is right there with and for us. The LORD placed us there. HE restores us there. HE anoints us there to Fly[141]!

Now the mighty prophet Isaiah spoke about rebellion, righteousness and the renewal of mankind. He knew there would be a time when we personally would go up to the mountain of the LORD. GOD would teach us of HIS ways, and we would walk in HIS paths[142]. That time is now. Your valley experiences have allowed you to move from all forms of rebellion to the mountain tops of righteousness. As you wait upon the LORD you are renewed

---

[137] Psalm 23:4

[138] 1 Samuel 17

[139] 2 Samuel 12

[140] 2 Samuel 24

[141] Psalm 23

[142] Isaiah 2:3

Chapter 11: Contraband: Slothfulness

and given wings as eagles[143]. Stop hiding in your church, you are ready to Fly.

To understand what happens when a Christian takes and doesn't give, I'll use the example of domesticated turkey. This bird has been systematically bred to NOT Fly. In America, we have a tradition of fattening turkeys up for the Thanksgiving Holiday so they will be nice, plump and juicy for the slaughter. These domesticated turkeys don't Fly; they feel good; look pretty; eat well; and remain safe in gated communities with turkeys like themselves.

Many Christians have chosen to be just like these domesticated turkeys, not working in GOD's vineyard. They are not sober or vigilant as the Bible mentions thus the devil is able to devour[144]. These Christians pose no threat to Satan because their interaction with sinners is minimal. They are slothful, easy targets, tasty to the enemy, and do not Fly. They live in what I call a gated church community. Nothing gets in without their approval.

GOD has given all Christians wings, but some Christians, much like the domesticated turkeys, don't Fly. They have chosen to be like these turkeys waiting for the "Second Coming" getting fatter and fatter in the religious ways. They are unable or unwilling to convert biblical information into true application.

These Christians are knowledge fat and weak in application. They are disconnected with the "SPIRIT of GOD." They believe, it's what they know, not what they apply which makes them a mature Christian. So they strut their stuff, looking so beautiful on the outside, but still very weak on the inside.

---

[143] Isaiah 40:31

[144] 1 Peter 5:8

Fly With GOD

They may never choose to affect the world and Fly. Somehow the "Awesome Truth" in the "Great Commission" to go out into the world, was missed.

They may go to church every day, but did they feed the hungry? How did they interact with their unbelieving co-workers or neighbors? Did they share all they ate with them or did they just show up the next Sunday morning to get more for themselves?

Better yet which of the two groups that passed the beaten man on the roadside in the parable of the "Good Samaritan[145]" best reflects their behavior? The Priest or the Levite? Remember, both groups were trained extensively in the Law. They seemed unaware of the grace and truth that came by JESUS CHRIST.

For this type of Christian, Thanksgiving Day will be when JESUS comes back for HIS servants. Will they have a place at the table? Will JESUS call them wicked servants? Or will they get crowns with no jewels?

I suspect by now, I have some readers disturbed about my comments about the real meaning of slothfulness. My remarks are focused only on a special type of believer, one which is equipped to go out into the world. The believer, who has chosen to disobey GOD's call on their life.

There are Christians who are not ready to yet. I believe there may be a point in someone's walk with JESUS that the "Awful Truth" is that they are so tired, hurt, and afraid that they need to take refuge in JESUS. This fear unlike the sinful fear that I discussed in the previous pages, is a godly fear. This is the type of fear mentioned in the Book of Psalms and Proverbs; the fear of the LORD. This type of fear leads to wisdom[146] and understanding of GOD's

---

[145]Luke 10:30-37

[146]James 1:4-5

Chapter 11: Contraband: Slothfulness

laws. It further states to ignore this type of fear is to be foolish and fall into evil.

This type of fear leads one to seek out the church, fellowship, and protection much like a toddler runs to their mother and father when strangers approach. This is a period when all boundaries have been possibly destroyed. They may not even know who they are anymore. The enemy may be in pursuit seeking to steal, and to kill, and to destroy them[147].

The "Awesome Truth" is that during this vulnerable time GOD holds them, protects them, and allows them to stay completely in HIS hands. GOD has allowed them this special time of rest. I call this rest time, Elijah—time, similar to when Elijah is under the Juniper tree and GOD takes care of his every need[148]. HE even gives him strength for a forty day journey to the mountain of GOD, Horeb. At this place the LORD calls Elijah back to Flight. The challenge with this picture is that GOD never meant for HIS people to stay in hiding.

This special time is meant for an appointed time. Just like baby chicks grow secure in their environment: begin to walk, run and then Fly. GOD has ordained the same for HIS people. If you have had an Elijah—time, it was meant to provide a deep healing for your soul. To allow you to become rooted in the love GOD has for you. It was to remind you that you are connected to the LIVING WATERS and that no matter what happens nothing can or will separate you from that life[149]. Like a toddler, fearlessly jumping off the table into the arms of their father, trusting he will catch them, trust GOD.

---

[147] John 10:10

[148] 1 Kings 19

[149] Jeremiah 2:13, 17:13, John 7:38

Fly With GOD

Vain Busyness

At the end of Luke 10, we find Martha upset with Mary for not helping her work. Martha accuses Mary of being slothful. JESUS rebukes Martha, telling her that Mary has chosen to do the best task. Here we see how easy it is to do a good thing, but not the best thing. Thus, slothfulness can be presented in many forms of busyness.

One way Christians miss the mark is to be so busy with the superficial work of the ministry that you miss the supernatural work of the presence of the SAVIOR. You fail to do what is most important.

To move from this type of slothfulness to where GOD is truly calling you, you will need to evaluate your desires. Are your desires of the flesh or of the SPIRIT? GOD can give you the ability to separate your flesh desires from your spiritual ones, and act on that knowledge. The sharp, two-edged sword in the Book of Hebrews allows the spirit within you to determine what is best for you at any moment[150].

How can you eliminate slothfulness? Slothfulness is eliminated one layer at a time. Much like the skin around an onion, we may have many layers of slothful behaviors. These layers will only be uncovered when we actually begin peeling away the areas GOD has called us to work on. Slothfulness truly requires the power of GOD as mentioned in Hebrews 4:12, "...that the Word of GOD is quick, and powerful, and sharper than any two-edged sword, piercing even to the dividing asunder of soul and spirit, and of the joints and marrow, and is a discerner of the thoughts and intents of the heart."

What is your labor motivated by? What "Awful Truth" and/or "Awesome Truth" is in you? The answers to these questions are found as you listen and act on the prodding of the HOLY SPIRIT.

---
[150]Hebrews 4:12

Chapter 11: Contraband: Slothfulness

In the Book of Jeremiah, we are told that if we seek GOD with all our heart we will find HIM and HE will bring us out of captivity [151]. I consider the labor that does not prosper us in the fashion GOD intended for us—to be captivity. Work for the sake of working may in fact be leading us further away from a fulfilling relationship with the CREATOR. Slothfulness for Christians must be defined as any labor that separates us from the best that GOD has for us.

GOD's desire is for us to be our most productive self; Holy-Action. As with the talents in the parable, HE expects a high return on HIS investment[152]. It is not enough to stay busy, but we must be about our FATHER's business. GOD is not concerned about quantity. HE has always been concerned about quality. The next scripture sums it up best.

Psalm 127:1

Except the LORD build the house, they labour in vain that build it: except the LORD keep the city, the watchman waketh but in vain.

This contraband really requires you to have a personal relationship with GOD. Nowhere in the Bible will you find the Flight plan for your journey. You have been specifically designed for your journey. Your uniqueness was designed to meet a very specific need on earth; a Holy-Action. If you doubt your uniqueness, try to find one person in the billions of people on earth that is just like you. Yes, you will find similar ones but none the same. You are truly irreplaceable. You are a fine instrument, your value increases when played by the best—our CREATOR.

That is why denying who you are or what you received from GOD has consequences. It may start with the little things, "like I can't do that", "that's not my strength", or "maybe later when I finish

---

[151] Jeremiah 29:11-15

[152] Matthew 25

Fly With GOD

this." It is deceptive, cunning, often shrouded in false humility (like Moses needing a spokesman or Barak needing Deborah) and more than willing to take on a form of godliness, but in reality it is you denying who GOD says you are, born to Fly.[153]

Matthew 5:14-16 (KJV)

Ye are the light of the world. A city that is set on an hill cannot be hid. Neither do men light a candle, and put it under a bushel, but on a candlestick; and it giveth light unto all that are in the house. Let your light so shine before men, that they may see your good works, and glorify your FATHER which is in heaven.

The world constantly tempts us to be slothful and hide our light, but the LORD calls us to let it shine. So you think you are too old or young, don't know enough; but GOD has chosen you. It no longer matters what the world has said about you. It doesn't even matter, what you say about you. It only matters what GOD says about you.

If GOD has chosen you to accomplish a task, HE will provide the resources to fulfill it. Fly, like the Apostle Paul, "I can do all things through CHRIST which strengtheneth me[154]." It is your time to listen to the HOLY SPIRIT, and then get up and do it. Don't let any task rest on your understanding. Your assignments must come from the LORD. HIS Word will accomplish that which HE has sent it to do.[155]

Don't let previous slothfulness stop your progress. You were not the first to eject in mid-air or to be hijacked. Jonah was swallowed by a whale while running from his assignment. Elijah hid in the cave fearing that Jezebel would kill him. Peter denied CHRIST three (3) times. But GOD directed each one of them back to their

---

[153]Exodus 4:10-16; Judges 4

[154]Philippians 4:13

[155]Isaiah 55:11

Chapter 11: Contraband: Slothfulness

mission. Their assignments were not canceled because of their failure to eliminate slothfulness. It was just delayed – until they got rid of the contraband. They finally listened to what GOD wanted them to pack. Their Holy-Action resumed when they eliminated slothfulness and sought their best.

GOD could have chosen anyone to replace Jonah, Elijah, and Peter, but HE didn't. The ALPHA, the OMEGA and the BEGINNING and the END determined their assignments. HE wasn't confused. HE didn't lack any information. HE chose them, knowing all about them, all their liabilities and assets. JESUS, the GOOD SHEPHERD, continued to pour out love, mercy and grace on them. HE led them out of darkness into the marvelous light. HE help them leave some of their contraband on the tarmac. HE chose them, just like HE chose you!

Please remember, no matter what you have done or not done, you can always start over. You are not the first to anger GOD after he gives you confirmation, after confirmation, after confirmation. When Moses, asked GOD, "how will they believe that YOU have sent me." GOD gave Moses three supernatural things. The first was a rod which could turn into a serpent. The second was his ability to change the color of his hand dramatically just by placing it under his shirt. The third was turning water into blood.[156] But Moses still wanted more. He angered GOD when he told the LORD he was not eloquent, but was slow in speech. GOD gave him Aaron to be his spokesman.

Talk to GOD share your apprehension and even your fears about the labor HE has asked you to do. HE will answer. HE may even provide you a surplus like HE did for Moses.

---

[156] Exodus 4:1-16

Dear LORD,

*Keep me busy with the activities that YOU uniquely created me for.
The tasks which show YOUR power and greatness to the universe.
Whether I am wavering or standing strong
let me keep my hand in YOUR hand.*

In JESUS CHRIST – Amen

Meditation Scriptures

- *Romans 12:11 (KJV) Not slothful in business; fervent in spirit; serving the LORD*

- *Hebrews 6:12 (KJV) That ye be not slothful, but followers of them who through faith and patience inherit the promises.*

- *Proverbs 10:4 (NIV) Lazy hands make a man poor, but diligent hands bring wealth.*

Chapter 11: Contraband: Slothfulness

Let your mind go from the superficial to the supernatural. What areas do you now believe GOD is calling you to? It is time we separate from the fair labor to GOD's best labor. Think about why you are not choosing GOD's best; how slothfulness is separating you from actually Flying? Then write it down. How are you hiding your light? How are you letting it shine?

Your Truth Time	
Awful: wicked and slothful	**Awesome: good and faithful**
1.	1.
2.	2.
3.	3.
4.	4.
5.	5.

Completion Date: ___/___/___

Chapter 12:
Contraband: Rebellion

REBELLION: Not doing what GOD said to do.

Is Rebellion your contraband? The "Awful Truth" is that in the beginning was rebellion. It is our oldest recorded contraband. It was first seen in the 3rd Chapter of Genesis when Adam and Eve resisted GOD's authority by eating the fruit. The carrying of this contraband led to humankind's expulsion from the Garden of Eden.

Any time you resist the direction of GOD in your life, you are in rebellion. The Bible provides you a long history of rebellion and its consequences from Genesis to Revelation. This is why even today Christians carry so much of it in their luggage.

What type of Rebellion. It is often hard for Christians to distinguish between godly and ungodly items when it comes to rebellion. We have become so comfortable with putting our spin on what GOD has asked us to do. Our ability to follow <u>exact</u> instruction has become extremely difficult. This contraband can be very deceiving and appear as godly luggage because it is "almost" what GOD said.

You must realize that if GOD instructs you to do it one way, that is the only way it should be done. HE does not require or need your input or anyone else's! Can you remember how Eve falsely responded to the serpent by saying even touching the

Chapter 12: Contraband: Rebellion

Tree-of-Knowledge-of-Good-and-Evil would bring death? That false information took mankind down a path full of more rebellion. We grew more and more accustomed to ad-libbing when it came to GOD's instructions.

The act of trying to sneak this contraband on board is not just limited to the ordinary Christian. It has affected the extraordinary Christian leaders throughout history. The Bible calls rebellion witchcraft[157] and rightly so; you need only look at Moses and Aaron to see the consequences of a rebellious act. They did not enter the Promised Land because they did not follow direct orders at the waters of Meribah[158].

The LORD had instructed them to speak to the rock and it would pour out its waters. Instead, Moses hit the rock twice. This ad-lib angered GOD to the point that both Moses and Aaron died without entering the Promised Land. What a costly ad-lib?

For King Saul, he sacrificed to GOD[159], but obeyed man. GOD had sent him to Amalek to kill all the people and destroy all their property. Instead, King Saul fearing the people – obeyed them instead of all of GOD's instructions. He captured King Agag and then sacrificed the best of the livestock to the LORD. Once again, just like Moses and Aaron, Saul defied GOD's instructions.

The Prophet Samuel uttered these famous lines to King Saul when he confronted him on his rebellion, "Obedience is better than sacrifice." King Saul's punishment for ad-libbing was that the LORD rejected him from being king over Israel. What a costly ad-lib?

Then there was the prophet who was obedient to GOD; except when a senior prophet intervened.[160] He was so anointed when

---

[157] 1 Samuel 15:23

[158] Numbers 20

[159] 1 Samuel 15

[160] 1 King 13

Fly With GOD

he prophesied to King Jeroboam, the king tried to grab him and GOD caused the king's hand to "dry-up". Later that same king has to come humbly to the prophet for a prayer of healing. The king requested that the prophet return with him for refreshments. The prophet rejected the worldly king's offer because the LORD had told the prophet to "eat no bread, nor drink water, nor turn again by the same way that thou camest."

In the same chapter, an old prophet (clearly a spiritual leader in the community), makes the same request to that prophet. The old prophet lies to him claiming an angel has spoken the word of the LORD, telling him to bring him back to his house for refreshments. The young prophet rebels against word GOD has personally given him and goes back to the old prophet's home. Shortly after, the young prophet is slain by a lion on the side of the road. What a costly ad-lib?

Then there is the prophetess Miriam's story. She rebelled against GOD's chosen leader Moses. She did not like the fact that he had chosen to marry an Ethiopian woman. Her prejudice led her to question Moses' authority (authority given by GOD). GOD was so angry with her that HE afflicted her with leprosy for seven days. What a costly ad-lib?

The contraband that these leaders had in their luggage was rebellion. Each of them experienced a different facet of the nature of rebellion and its consequences. Moses not following <u>exact</u> instructions; King Saul caring more about what people would say or do; the prophet believing a "man of God", instead of GOD; and finally prophetess Miriam afflicted by prejudice. So when, GOD speaks to us, our feelings, what people think, say or do – <u>don't matter</u>. We need to listen to HIM and immediately follow HIS instructions and Fly.

How can you eliminate Rebellion? Rebellion is eliminated when we are obedient to the "Word" GOD has for us. By one man's rebellion we were made sinners, but by the obedience of one man, JESUS CHRIST, we are made righteous.

So the "Awesome Truth" is that you have a way out, you don't have to live in rebellion. For many of us the clarity of that statement is unclear; what does GOD want us to do next? It is not that we want to disobey; it is that we are not sure what we should be doing. We've not developed habits that allow us to be sure of HIS voice. GOD's instructions can come in so many different ways. We have to be constantly available to HIS call.

If our relationship is weak in any dimension we may not hear HIM clearly. We may miss HIS full instructions. The following passage is a reminder that in order to hear GOD's voice we may have to be still, wait, watch and listen.

1 Kings 19:11-13 (KJV)

And he said, Go forth, and stand upon the mount before the LORD. And, behold, the LORD passed by, and a great and strong wind rent the mountains, and brake in pieces the rocks before the LORD; but the LORD was not in the wind: and after the wind an earthquake; but the LORD was not in the earthquake: And after the earthquake a fire; but the LORD was not in the fire: and after the fire a still small voice.

What will it actually sound like for you? I don't know; with that answer you may be ready to close the book, but wait a minute, I know who does. It is you. Yes, You! JESUS promised, that HE would send the HOLY SPIRIT to all that confessed with their mouths that, "JESUS is LORD," and believe in their hearts that GOD raised HIM from the dead.[161] So if you have done that, the COUNSELOR will teach you all things. HE will remind you of everything JESUS has said to you. Through your relationship with the LORD, you will be

---

[161]Roman 9:10

Fly With GOD

able to recognize the sound of HIS voice even in a crowd and be able to obey.

My favorite example of just that; is to watch a child call "Mommy" in a crowded store. It doesn't matter if the child is two or 42; mothers are always able to recognize their child's voice. Why? the child and mother have a special birth bond. They communicate with their hearts, eyes, body, soul and speech. They may not always agree; but they definitely communicate. GOD has that same birth bond with you, if you will incline your ear.[162]

If you feel you need a breakthrough in your communication skills with GOD, then call HIM. My personal favorite call comes from Jeremiah "...*GOD's message, the GOD who made earth, made it livable and lasting, known everywhere as GOD "Call to me and I will answer you. I'll tell you marvelous and wondrous things that you could never figure out on your own[163]."* I like to pray using this passage because I am constantly humbled by what GOD will reveal to me if I will only surrender and ask.

A broken spirit and a contrite heart in a person that is willing to fall on their knees and say "HELP," always gets answers from GOD. Praise GOD, HE has never been caught up in the words, but in our heart. Just calling on the Name of JESUS is enough for HIM to reveal your next step.

You are never far from being enticed into a rebellious act no matter how mature your Christian walk. Rebellion can occur in a split second, you must continue to maintain your fellowship with JESUS to receive your "instructional updates." Corinthians tells us to not only cast down any imagination that is against the knowledge of GOD, but to capture every thought making it obedient to CHRIST.[164]

---

[162]Proverbs 4:19-21 (KJV)

[163]Jeremiah 33:2-3 (MSG)

[164]2 Corinthians 10:5-7

Once you are in the habit of being obedient to CHRIST, you will be ready to defeat every act of rebellion. As obedience becomes a habit, GOD will truly be a lamp unto your feet and show you what *"instructional adjustments"* HE is making daily, if not, second-by-second.

You need only to review the story of Gideon[165] to be reminded that it is OK to ask GOD for daily instructional updates especially when the task requires a battle. Here, you find Gideon an obedient servant of the LORD. He is from a poor family, where he is the least among them. But Gideon is used to save Israel.

What makes him a great example for us is that he keeps asking the LORD to do something special, so that he is confident that he is actually hearing from GOD. When, GOD instructs him to defeat the Midianites, he asks GOD to confirm HIS command by wetting a fleece on the floor, while the actual floor remains dry. GOD does just that. Gideon requires more proof. He asks GOD, not to be upset with him, but to do the opposite the next morning. GOD answers his request. Here we see that GOD knew that Gideon wanted to be obedient. The confirmation of GOD's instruction was all he needed in order to Fly. The passage ended with Gideon Flying in obedience to what GOD reveals.

Now it is time for you to dig deep and think about areas of rebellion in your life. Where are you still ad-libbing when it comes to GOD's instructions in your life? Is it at work, home, or church? Are you still caring more about what people will say or do to you, then GOD? Are you letting people in the ministry: family friends, pastors, bishops, and others determine the instructions you follow, not GOD? Or finally, is some prejudice stopping you from being obedient?

There was a time when the church was very powerful. It was during that period when the early Christians rejoiced when

---

[165] Judges 6 and 7

they were deemed worthy to suffer for what they believed. In those days the church was not merely a thermometer that recorded the ideas and principles of popular opinion; it was a thermostat that transformed the mores of society. Whenever the early Christians entered a town the power structure got disturbed and immediately sought to convict them for being "disturbers of the peace" and "outside agitators." But they went on with the conviction that they were "a colony of heaven," and had to obey GOD rather than man. They were small in number but big in commitment. They were too GOD-intoxicated to be "astronomically intimidated." They brought an end to such ancient evils as infanticide and gladiatorial contest.

Martin Luther King Letter from Birmingham Jail (April 1963)

Dear LORD,

Help me to hear YOUR voice and respond quickly to YOUR command.
Allow me to live a life where doing YOUR will second-by-second is the most important thing to me.
Thank you In JESUS Name

Meditation Scriptures

- *Romans 6:16 (KJV) Know ye not, that to whom ye yield yourselves servants to obey, his servants ye are to whom ye obey; whether of sin unto death, or of obedience unto righteousness?*

- *2 Corinthians 10:5 (KJV) Casting down imaginations, and every high thing that exalteth itself against the knowledge of GOD, and bringing into captivity every thought to the obedience of CHRIST;*

Chapter 12: Contraband: Rebellion

Spend some time reflecting on how obedient you are to GOD at home, work, church, and your community. Complete the chart.

Your Truth Time	
Awful: Rebellion	**Awesome: Obedience**
Home	Home
Work	Work
Church	Church
Community	Community

Completion Date: ___/___/___

Chapter 13: Other Contraband

OTHER CONTRABAND – Other actions, behaviors, habits, and incidents which do not line-up with the grace and truth of JESUS CHRIST.

This is where you write your own customized chapter. I told you earlier about how special you are. Your uniqueness may have led to some highly specialized contraband. What other contraband has GOD revealed to you while reading the previous chapters?

Now is your chance to explain, list the contraband, check the category it falls under, and if you know the cause list it also.

Chapter 13: Other Contraband

Describe the Contraband	People	Places	Things	Other	What is the root cause GOD has revealed to you?

Completion Date: ___/___/___

Fly With GOD

Dear JESUS CHRIST,

Thank YOU for revealing YOUR truth to me right now. I joyously give YOU permission to work on me. I will run towards YOUR truth. Open my eyes LORD that I may see the truth YOU have for me. Give me the strength and skills to apply the truth YOU reveal, moment-by-moment.

Finally, keep me in the center of YOUR will working on my contraband in the order that YOU have assigned. Let me be patient and willing to allow YOU the Potter to shape and mold me; and no one else. Protect me, even if it has to be from me. Wash me continuously in YOUR BLOOD.

In JESUS Name I pray.

Meditation Scriptures

- *Philippians 1:6 (KJV) Being confident of this very thing, that HE which hath begun a good work in you will perform it until the day of JESUS CHRIST:*

Part 4: Terminal

The only thing more expensive than education is ignorance.

— Benjamin Franklin

You're Finally Ready To Fly

Your bags are packed and have been processed. It is now time for you to go to the terminal, through security and proceed to the departure gate.

Do you have all your bags?

Do you have your license?

Do you have your passport?

Do have your flight plan?

Do you have a manifest?

Chapter 14: Check-in

CHECK-IN: The place where you believe you have released enough baggage to Fly.

Where is the Terminal to Check-in? The "Terminal" is the place where we find our-self with the LORD having either surrendered or yielded to HIS will. The place where we come to our senses, where we desire more than good, we desire GOD's best!

You may have survived exile or partial separation from GOD, but you're here. Getting to the terminal can be instantaneous like Enoch's journey or can take over 40 years like the children of Israel. Terminal Check-in is a sweet place where GOD is talking and you are finally at a place where you are listening.

Check-in time means you're available for flying solo in spirit and actions. A tremendous amount of contraband has already been left behind. You have made significant improvements in your spiritual journey. You have a heightened ability to listen and act on the things of GOD. Habits have been developed which allow you to quickly and skillfully dismiss the naysayers and care only about what GOD instructs.

Your transformation now qualifies you to Fly solo. You no longer require the blessings of others to accomplish the assignment GOD

Fly With GOD

gave you. Christian maturity allows you to be willing and able to Fly solo with no one else. You are completely GOD-dependent. This GOD–dependent state also means that you lean not on your own understanding but on GOD[166] for your progress.

Each person on this planet has a unique call on their life with their own personalized journey. Each journey has a unique start and finish line determined by the LORD.

You may think it is unfair that you have to Fly solo, with a different starting line? You may even notice that your starting line is further back? Don't be concerned about these differences. The LORD says HE will judge your progress. HE searches the heart, tries it, and rewards you based on what HE sees.[167] Being GOD–dependent allows you and me to focus only on GOD's directions to Fly.

Whether flight Check-in causes you excitement, pain, or discomfort, you need to purpose in your heart what GOD said. HE says you were born to Fly and the HOLY SPIRIT has prepared you for this moment. It is time not only to Check-in, but to review the manifest. You will find your name on it, along with folks like Abraham, David, Samuel, Ruth, Esther, Peter, and Paul; just to name a few good pilots.

Time to hand the attendant at the curb your credentials. She reminds you of the weight guidelines for your baggage. Praise GOD! You have just read the previous chapters and have done all you can to eliminate extra baggage.

As the attendant indicates your boarding gate, you notice out of the corner of your eye a gentleman that clearly has exceeded the baggage limits. The contraband is actually sticking out from every side of his baggage. The attendant is looking at him as if he is a psychiatric patient. He is ranting about how the additional baggage is critical for his journey. He is pulling out more and more money

---

[166] Proverbs 3:4-6

[167] Jeremiah 17:8-10

Chapter 14: Check-in

(for many of you this is the time you start talking about your good works, awards accolades) trying to pay for the extra weight. The attendant just keeps shaking her head, NO.

You think to yourself, "Is he really that naive? Does he realize the actual cost of carrying that much extra baggage on his flight?" You're feeling glad you're not him. Doesn't he know the "Awful Truth" that the extra baggage will keep him chained to the ground? He's in bondage and doesn't even know it. His plane won't be able to take off or even worst crash after take-off! You look over again, and he is discarding some of the contraband. The attendant is telling him, "It is still not enough," if he wants to Fly.

This gentleman was at the Check-in area but was not prepared for his journey. I'm sure he thought he was ready to Fly, but he had not completed the actions necessary to eliminate his contraband. I wonder if he was like that rich man in Matthew, not willing to sell his possession and give to the poor.[168]

People like this gentleman, if they ever get in the air, will find they are unable to maintain any meaningful altitude if they do not change. They may even complain about how bumpy their lives have been since they met CHRIST. They don't listen and are unwilling to leave their contraband at the gate. They will never soar, because they have exceeded their weight limit. They did not leave the things holding them down behind. They are still chained to their past or to someone else's future.

The "Awful Truth" is that all of the self-help books and self-talk exercises have failed to alter their behavior. These individuals still have too much contraband. The contraband weighing down their luggage can only be eliminated with the power of the HOLY SPIRIT. They may have spent years disposing of the smallest pieces while the boulders in their baggage remained untouched. Their position at the Check-in window does not matter. They are still holding the

---

[168] Matthew 19:21

Fly With GOD

items that GOD said to let go of. Until they let go of those items, their flights have been delayed.

The "Awesome Truth" is that the Check-in window points to GOD.[169] Brother or sister, if you still have some contraband that needs to go, HIS stretched-out hand is waiting to help you eliminate the contraband. Whether you started obeying HIS voice early in your life, in the middle, or in your twilight years, HE still has a plan for you to eliminate contraband and Fly.

What you are willing to walk away from at the Check-in window will determine what GOD will give you next. Your continuous relationship with JESUS will give you the power to leave the contraband and replace it with treasure as you continue on.

As we move through the Check-in area toward security, we notice a strong foul smell. There is a massive pile of baggage just before security. People from all over the Check-in area are lining up to add more and more to the piles of baggage. We can't believe the kinds of articles that are being piled up to the ceiling. It seems like millions and millions of items have found their way to this area. We finally look up to see a gigantic sign. It is the largest sign we have ever seen. It has but one word on it.

BURDENS

Those seven large letters may bring tears to our eyes. If we remember the truth. The fear, the hurt, and finally the pain, and how it eventually turned into hope gratitude and joy. Thank goodness, we made the righteous choices and left ours behind. We couldn't have stood another line. We're ready to go through security now.

Security. Who does GOD say you are? You are faced with an "Awful Truth;" it is time for you to go through the Security Gate.

---
[169]Luke 11:9

Chapter 14: Check-in

NO problem, right? YES, big problem! The heart[170] of man is so wicked that only GOD can truly search it and determine its ways. That is why whether you know it or not, you are about to set off every alarm in the place, unless you are a VIP – that is, Very Important Person. For the non-VIPs, the sound will be excruciating. This sound will pale to the shame felt once they realize that they will have to be searched possibly in front of everyone, including family, friends and foes. This search won't be a simple pat down or even a strip search, but a full body cavity search to ensure that nothing has been missed.

I personally have fought my whole life not to expose everything. The thought of being naked in front of anyone, let alone body cavity search, what a violation. Just the thought of it makes me cringe. I can understand it if you are starting to feel a bit apprehensive about this security process—especially the lengths and depths you must go through to Fly. "No one is supposed to be that vulnerable," is what I used to say! I'm just keeping a few secrets to myself. Come on …doesn't the Bible tell us to bridle our tongue?

We must understand that security has to verify our identity. They must make sure we are who we say we are and no one else is slipping through on our credentials. All those dark areas in our life will have to be exposed for security purposes.

NO MORE SECRETS

When I look back at my journey, I realized I didn't understand the security process. Even though I had eliminated some major contraband, I still wasn't sure who I really was; much less who GOD was calling me to be. So I would hide from people, but the greatest tragedy was I was hiding from myself. I had forgotten the truth about how "fearfully and wonderfully"[171] I was made

---

[170]Jeremiah 17:9

[171]Psalm 139:14

Fly With GOD

by HIM. How much I want to be loved for who I am. How much I had hidden my truest desires for fear that if I asked GOD, all HIS answers might be NO.

So one day, as I prepared to go through security, I realized an Awesome Truth, GOD knows who I am. HE is waiting for me to say who I am. Until I was willing to reveal me-to-me, the COMFORTER waited as a patient teacher for me to get the answer right. Waiting for me to be naked and not ashamed. I finally asked GOD to search my heart and show me who I was, who I am, and who I am called to be. As I did, I reflected on King David's plea:

> *"Search me, O GOD, and know my heart: try me, and know my thoughts: and see if there be any wicked way in me, and lead me."*[172]

Like many, when GOD revealed it, I tried to run from those images HE showed me. Those same images, I know HE will show you. Don't run! Please be smarter than me and skip the pain and anguish; just surrender; enjoy the ride. Follow the COMFORTER like I eventually did and go to the VIP area.

We are so important to GOD. What HE shows us, if we let HIM, is our new improved status. For us, Flying is about the grace and mercy GOD has in store for us. This grace and mercy creates an area where we receive special treatment from the LORD. Here, HE further equips us to succeed. The Awesome Truth is that in this area, GOD has changed our status to VIPs.

Earlier, I gave you the Awful Truth about alarms and nakedness, but here is the Awesome Truth, JESUS CHRIST left us with the HOLY SPIRIT to be our powerful guide. This guide, when followed, allows us to go through the security gate marked for VIPs only. Your passport reads, "Blood of JESUS, led by the HOLY SPIRIT;" you get special treatment. All because HE has made you righteous.

---

[172] Psalms 139:22-24 (KJV)

Chapter 14: Check-in

This treatment allows you to go through security to a special 1-on-1 briefing area. There you will be screened by your personal trainer "the COMFORTER." HE will coach you through your own customized "contraband disposal program." This program does not require you to be contraband free in order to Fly. It is a program based on doing what GOD says to do when HE says to do it. Its only requirement for receiving GOD's mercy and grace is that you follow the "COMFORTER's" instructions. As long as you eliminate the additional items when ordered to, you will be able to obtain lift-off and Fly.

You are listening to GOD's orders. The contraband you once wore or carried with you no longer matters. They falsely define who you are. You may have been stuck in your same stuff so long that it not only smells, but it is stuck to you. You are now able to take it off with the COMFORTER's assistance.

As you pass through the final moments of security, you suddenly realize how much the COMFORTER has helped you. You are standing there naked. You are not too cold or too hot. You are not profiling or hiding. You are just standing in the flight suit of GOD.[173] You begin to no longer care about people's opinions or actions.

You think to yourself, this is what it must have felt like before the fall of Adam and Eve. As the COMFORTER continues to assist you in the timely disposal of the contraband, like fear, disbelief, unforgiveness, slothfulness, rebellion, and the others; HE fills the empty spaces with GOD's holiness, which only the FATHER of the Universe can give you.

> HE fills the empty space of fear with "Truth"
> HE fills the empty space of disbelief with "Faith"
> HE fills the empty space of unforgiveness with "Forgiveness"
> HE fills the empty space of slothfulness with the "Holy Action"
> *HE fills the empty space of rebellion with "Obedience"*

---

[173] Ephesians 6:10-20

Fly With GOD

The SAVIOR is there to fill empty bags with precious jewels. Luke chapter 11 provides a reminder of the dangers of leaving the bags empty after the contraband has been disposed of. It states, if the bag is left empty, eventually seven more dangerous contrabands will arrive and occupy the bag.[174]

GOD has always desired your final condition to be better than the initial condition. Your heaviness and pain is now being replaced with GOD's VIP Rewards Program. A VIP Rewards Program, which is based on a flight suit of truth, righteousness, peace, faith, salvation, GOD's Word and prayer.[175]

We have finally surrendered and are filled with GOD's rewards. We are standing before our FATHER "naked and not ashamed," no matter what our resume looks like or our current frailties. We can enjoy GOD's promises like Adam and Eve did in the beginning of their fellowship. We finally experience what it is to be safe and secure in our nakedness, with our bags filled by GOD to the brim!

Precious LORD,

Thank you for YOUR mercy and grace. When I stay connected with YOU all things work together for good in my life.

Help me to come boldly to the throne. Let me leave my burdens at the altar. GOD, allow me to put on YOUR robe of righteousness and carry out YOUR orders.

In JESUS name – Amen

---

[174] Luke 11:24-26
[175] Ibid

Chapter 14: Check-in

Meditation Scriptures

- *Psalm 51:6-7 (KJV) Behold, thou desirest truth in the inward parts: and in the hidden part thou shalt make me to know wisdom. Purge me with hyssop, and I shall be clean: wash me, and I shall be whiter than snow.*

- *Hebrews 4:15-17 (KJV) For we have not an high priest which cannot be touched with the feeling of our infirmities; but was in all points tempted like as we are, yet without sin. Let us therefore come boldly unto the throne of grace, that we may obtain mercy, and find grace to help in time of need.*

Fly With GOD

Now it's truth time again. How is your baggage now? What more did you leave behind as you went through security? What do you need to keep?

Complete the "Your Truth Time" exercise below. Write as much as you can. This is only a snapshot—GOD will reveal much more at your appointed[176] time.

Your Truth Time (Complete each section. Use more paper if necessary)	
Awful	**Awesome**
People	People
Place	Place
Things	Things

**Completion Date: ___/___/___ - 3rd Time

** *You will see this form again, each time adding or subtracting information based on revelation and knowledge from the LORD. Be sure to date your entries so that you can chart your progress.*

---

[176] Habakkuk 2:3

Chapter 15: Waiting Room

WAITING ROOM: Is the place where all the right conditions come together in order for you to Fly.

The "Waiting Room" is the place where our faith in the LORD has the potential to soar if we not only surrender but yield to HIS entire will for our lives. In Habakkuk, we are told that, *"The vision is yet for an appointed time, but at the end it shall speak, and not lie: though it tarry, wait for it; because it will surely come, it will not tarry."*[177]

You have been given glimpses of your personal flight plan and now it is time for you to "Wait For It." This is your season[178] to study, your time for developing patience and a time for upgrades. It may seem like it is taking too long, but remember, feeling ready and acting ready does not equal being ready.

This is your season for preparation. It "will not tarry" because it will appear when you are truly ready. The very instant the weather conditions and the equipment say you are ready, you will be given the green light to Fly; and not a second before or after! So get READY!

---

[177] Habakkuk 2:3

[178] Ecclesiastes 3:1-8

> **It is a mistake to try to look too far ahead. The chain of destiny can only be grasped one link at a time.**
>
> **Sir Winston Churchill**

Aircraft Upgrades. Whether you are a passenger or a pilot, you must still pass the same level of inspection revealed in the previous chapters in order to Fly. GOD's desire is for you to transition from passenger in those large jumbo jets to pilot in something like a super hornet. The Waiting Room is the place where the transitions take place; the place where GOD provides you with supernatural opportunities; I call them plane upgrades.

GOD will send people into your life to do favors for you. And because it is unmerited favor, you may become suspicious of their motives, but don't be; you are flowing in GOD's grace. Don't worry about why the person is helping you; just praise GOD and remember where your blessings come from.

Trust that GOD knows what's in the hearts of these individuals—not us. If their motives are not right, HE will take care of them. It is also a place where you meet a range of other flyers; ranging from wannabes to expert fighter pilots. This is the place where GOD may upgrade your aircraft from a "glider" to a "space shuttle." Finally, it is where your faith is matured through action by following GOD's commands.

This is where your spiritual discernment will reveal the "Posers," the pilots who have not actually flown a plane; the pilots that imitate well but have not yet achieved any flight success. The posers have no real testimony. They can tell lengthy stories about how others have accomplished their journeys, but they personally have no expertise of their own.

These posers are dangerous because they have never flown. Their advice can appear to be very spiritual, but in reality, it comes from sources ranging from milk Christians to false prophets. They often

Chapter 15: Waiting Room

lurk around hoping to vicariously experience the soaring effects that true pilots experience. Some may pose as your closest friends hoping to ride the wave of your anointing, if you let them. They have not yet realized that there is only a prize for the pilots who actually Fly.

The Waiting Room is where your aircraft type is determined. In the natural, a jet plane, space shuttle, glider, or helicopter is capable of flying through the air. Your spiritual journey has a similar supernatural framework but its flying is done in heavenly places. You may start the journey off in a glider, but eventually end up in a super hornet. The choice is always determined by your obedience to the HOLY SPIRIT.

Your plane type will be determined by the amount of baggage you are still carrying and your adherence to the directions given by the "COMFORTER." There are all types of aircrafts you can use for either your natural or spiritual journey. To help you understand the similarities, I have included the table on the next page. The table indicates a few aircraft types and compares their natural and supernatural features.

Aircraft	Features
Glider	***Natural:*** A plane without a motor; light weight; used for moving in the air from a higher to a lower level by gravity or from a lower to a higher level by air currents. Rains, winds and storms easily damage them. ***Supernatural:*** Spiritually light weight; they do not handle conflict well. Christians that have not transitioned from baby food to meat; require assistance in steering. Tendency to go where the wind and/or gravity of the situation (other Christians and or people) take them. Every time a new person shows up in this person's life they change their direction. They adapt to people, places and things instead of to the LORD.
Jumbo Jet (747)	***Natural:*** One of the largest passenger aircrafts; four engines; with the capacity to carry 500 passengers and their baggage. ***Supernatural:*** Heavy weight spiritual planes designed to carry huge amounts of people, places and things; they can handle light conflict but no major battles. They have not been willing to leave behind baggage and passengers. They love the LORD but are still crowd pleasers; trying to help everybody. They often carry religious doctrine and do plenty of good works. Their strong belief in doctrine allows them to be over occupied with law and less occupied with a relationship with JESUS. Their plane is full with all the rules but not much of the love, mercy and grace of JESUS CHRIST that would set them free and allow them to Fly high.

Chapter 15: Waiting Room

Super Hornet	**Natural:** A single or two-seated, twin engine, multi-mission fighter/attack aircraft that can operate from either aircraft carriers or land bases. It has air superiority, fighter escort, suppression of enemy air defenses, reconnaissance, forward air control, close and deep air support, and day and night strike missions. It has a flight control system which provides excellent handling qualities, and allows pilots to learn to fly the airplane with relative ease. This system provides exceptional maneuverability and allows the pilot to concentrate on operating the weapons system. A solid thrust-to-weight ratio and superior turn characteristics combined with energy sustainability, enable it to hold its own against any adversary. **Supernatural:** Light weight spiritual fighter planes designed to quickly attack and defeat spiritual wickedness in high places without compromising its pilot's mission. They can take direct spiritual hits, recover successfully (free of depression), repair quickly, and fly again the next day. They have a proven survivability record (their testimonies support that they have been through unbelievable tests). They carry only two passengers (Pilot & COMFORTER) and very little carry-on luggage. They are what the Epistles of Peter mention when it encourages Christians to be excellent fighters, great in self-defense, and fighting the attacks of the false ministry pilots. This tactical aircraft is always available to handle any type of spiritual warfare.

Fly With GOD

You have been given a vision for your flight plan, and the plan is a promise from GOD, but you may still have to wait patiently for the details before boarding your aircraft. That waiting patiently can be your biggest test.

As you wait, you will see other pilots take off. Pilots you might have trained, supported, and prayed with for months, if not for years; even pilots that have taken your pearls and have allowed spiritual amnesia to stop them from giving you credit. I have been there, I have felt the pain of seemingly unanswered prayers; but when it was all said and done, I had to be reminded just like Job[179] where was I when GOD laid the earth's foundation? What knowledge do I have unless GOD gives it to me? Thus, I must wait, and so must you.

Patience. So why must we wait? We have the plane, we have our flight plan, and we even have the promise from GOD! The Apostle James answers this question best when he says, *"Because the trying of our faith works patience; perfecting us...so we want for nothing."*[180] It seems the Bible is full of stories of individuals much like us, being further prepared while they waited for the promise.

Caleb waited over 40 years to obtain the promise of the high ground and the land of milk and honey. Joseph waited over 20 years in slavery for the promise to rule over his brothers. Esther waited over twelve months for the promise to become queen and the disciples waited in the upper room for 50 days for the COMFORTER that JESUS promised.

No matter how spiritual they were, nothing happened before its time. They all had to develop more patience. The "Awesome Truth" is that the wait may have varied; the preparation may have varied; but the promise never varied, it was always true.

---

[179] Job 38

[180] James 1:3-4

Chapter 15: Waiting Room

There are also stories of not waiting patiently and the consequences of rushing GOD's promise. At 75 years old, GOD promised Abraham many heirs.[181] At 86 years old, he was still heirless, so he agreed with his wife to help GOD by having a child with her servant Hagar. At 100 years old, he received the promise—Isaac; but by this time, his actions had caused strife not only in his household, but the rippling effects are still being felt today.

In the New Testament, we find Barnabas[182] wanting to take Mark[183] with him and Paul, to minister in Syria and Cilicia. Paul refuses to take Mark with them because of his impatient behavior. Mark had deserted Paul in Pamphylia. Paul selects Silas instead; and they go on to many spiritual victories and Mark's victories are delayed.

Then, there was the moaning and grumbling that took place as Moses brought the children of Israel out of bondage to the land with milk and honey. These grumblings led to a journey that extended more than 40 years until the death of all of the rebellious adults.

If Abraham, Mark and the children of Israel had problems being patient after seeing firsthand the mighty miracles from GOD, how can we remain patient? Because we have much more "the COMFORTER"! JESUS left us the HOLY SPIRIT that resides inside of us. Most of the Old Testament followers did not have that gift. This gift allows us to have an attitude of joy no matter what comes our way, we have the victory. As mentioned earlier,[184] James 1:3-4, reminds us of how trying our faith works patience but verse 2[185] tells us about our attitudes. These tests and challenges are a gift and we should embrace them with joy. If we know, GOD's promise,

---

[181] Genesis 12:4
[182] Acts 15:37-41
[183] John nicknamed Mark
[184] James 1:3-4 (KJV, MSG)
[185] James 1:2 (KJV, MSG)

Fly With GOD

that something truly special is coming. We can wait with joy to inherit the promise.[186]

I believe what we are waiting for are brilliant and priceless diamonds in the spiritual realm. We are being perfected during very specific conditions. Just like natural diamonds begin as coal that under exposure to specific conditions are transformed; spiritual diamonds require tribulations, trials and challenges for our transformation.

In the natural, these pressures produce a hard, transparent, almost flawless piece of stone, but in the spiritual realm it produces faith, patience, hope, and finally, leaving us wanting for nothing. This formation process allows us to become a fine-cutting tool facing all obstacles with precision, while all the time reflecting GOD's brilliant light.

What is even more interesting is that in the natural a diamond's worth is based on a clarity grading to determine whether it has any inclusions and/or blemishes visible to a skilled grader using 10x magnification. But in the spiritual realm our clarity is based on our ability to reflect GOD's light. This requires the Word; there is no way around it.

The Word is the only solution to an impatient nature. In this, *Fast Food –Technological* era, making the time to stay in the Word is critical to developing and keeping patience. I have included some of my favorite scriptures to assist you in those times when you want to scream, "Let me Fly now!" Hopefully, you will put them in your spiritual emergency kit.

---

[186]Hebrews 6:12

Verse	Detail from King James Version (KJV)
Psalm 37:7	Rest in the LORD, and wait patiently for him: fret not thyself because of him who prospereth in his way, because of the man who bringeth wicked devices to pass.
Psalm 127:1-2	Except the LORD build the house, they labour in vain that build it: except the LORD keep the city, the watchman waketh but in vain. It is vain for you to rise up early, to sit up late, to eat the bread of sorrows: for so he giveth his beloved sleep.
Luke 8:15	But that on the good ground are they, which in an honest and good heart, having heard the Word, keep it, and bring forth fruit with patience.
Romans 5:3-5	And not only so, but we glory in tribulations also: knowing that tribulation worketh patience; And patience, experience; and experience, hope: And hope maketh not ashamed; because the love of GOD is shed abroad in our hearts by the Holy Ghost which is given unto us.

Verse	Detail from King James Version (KJV)
Romans 8:24-26	For we are saved by hope: but hope that is seen is not hope: for what a man seeth, why doth he yet hope for? But if we hope for that we see not, then do we with patience wait for it. Likewise the Spirit also helpeth our infirmities: for we know not what we should pray for as we ought: but the Spirit itself maketh intercession for us with groanings which cannot be uttered.
Romans 15:3-5	For even CHRIST pleased not himself; but, as it is written, The reproaches of them that reproached thee fell on me. For whatsoever things were written aforetime were written for our learning, that we through patience and comfort of the scriptures might have hope. Now the GOD of patience and consolation grant you to be likeminded one toward another according to CHRIST JESUS:
Galatians 6:9-10	And let us not be weary in well doing: for in due season we shall reap, if we faint not. As we have therefore opportunity, let us do good unto all men, especially unto them who are of the household of faith.
Hebrews 6:12	That ye be not slothful, but followers of them who through faith and patience inherit the promises

Chapter 15: Waiting Room

Verse	Detail from King James Version (KJV)
Hebrews 10:35-39	Cast not away therefore your confidence, which hath great recompense of reward. For ye have need of patience, that, after ye have done the will of GOD, ye might receive the promise. For yet a little while, and he that shall come will come, and will not tarry.
Hebrews 12:1-3	Wherefore seeing we also are compassed about with so great a cloud of witnesses, let us lay aside every weight, and the sin which doth so easily beset us, and let us run with patience the race that is set before us, Looking unto JESUS the author and finisher of our faith; who for the joy that was set before him endured the cross, despising the shame, and is set down at the right hand of the throne of GOD. For consider him that endured such contradiction of sinners against himself, lest ye be wearied and faint in your minds.
James 1:2-4	My brethren, count it all joy when ye fall into divers temptations; Knowing this, that the trying of your faith worketh patience. But let patience have her perfect work, that ye may be perfect and entire, wanting nothing.

Fly With GOD

Study. It is your responsibility as a present or future pilot to be prepared for all flights by studying the Operations Manual–the Bible. Here you find out how to effectively use all GOD's resources for lift-off and soaring. This is the time GOD gives you to obtain, understand, and apply all available spiritual information found in your Operational Manual. The Waiting Room is the best place to find out if you are teachable; it is where your study habits are perfected. This is where reading, writing, and arithmetic become essential to your Flight. The skills you perfect during this process will determine the type of pilot you will become. Robotic memorization of your Operational Manual will not do; your study must be girded with the HOLY SPIRIT. Only with the HOLY SPIRIT will you receive the wisdom and power to Fly.

The information from your Bible studies, daily devotionals, meditation, and prayers are the substances used to create that clean heart. What is studied during the Waiting Room experience will save your life. When Timothy said, "Study to shew thyself approved unto GOD, a workman that needeth not to be ashamed, rightly dividing the Word of truth,"[187] he was not only reminding you of the value of studying the Word to determine truth, but the consequences of not studying, including the shame.

For you and I, there is nothing more embarrassing then falling flat on our face in front of others, especially when we could have avoided it if we took the time to study. Studying allows GOD to open up HIS secrets to you so that you will be prepared when the time comes to use that knowledge.

If you are one of those Christians which are still thinking about not really studying the Operation Manual–the Bible–or possibility skimming it for the good parts and studying only those, you will be completely unprepared for your flight.

---

[187] 2 Timothy 2:15

Chapter 15: Waiting Room

The weather conditions while in the air can change quickly. One minute you're cruising along in sunny skies, the next moment you are in a thunderstorm; praying every second. At that moment, what you studied during your Waiting Room experience could be the very thing that saves your life and many others.

How many times have you gotten new equipment and read the operational manual? Or gone on a trip and read the entire brochure? Let's be honest, if you read 10% of the book or brochure you really felt you were knowledgeable. I personally like the skimming approach looking only for the warnings. But flying is a life or death matter. It is not the time to be reading the operational manual while the plane is in a nose dive. What is in your heart at that moment will govern your brain and thus your actions.

Several years ago, I heard a story about a software vendor who brought more than a 100 people together to test the loading of their new software product. They asked the participants to read the instructions and load the new software. They had figured this session would take several hours. They had all the conditions just right; terrific environment, great hotel, chairs, desks, clear monitors, the best computers. But they quickly had to end the project.

They had not considered the human factor. The factor that no matter how many warnings you give, a human's nature to be impatient may lead them to dangerous short cuts. As the individuals read the instructions given to them on that day, only one person followed the directions; the rest of them erased the entire information on their computer, ending the test. Is it wrong for me to hope that a Christian would have fallen into that 1% and read the instructions?

It seems that any device you buy these days needs a manual; the more complex the device, the more technical the operational manual. Some devices include manuals with their own self-paced computerized tutorials; others give you a list of consultants who will make house calls to help you. It shouldn't surprise you that the

Fly With GOD

most complex device on earth—you—comes with an operational manual and a 24/7 personal guide to insure that you operate under the specifications indicated by YOUR inventor.

The Bible is the Operations Manual for the most complex device in the world—that is you. There is no situation you can get into that the Bible along with the HOLY SPIRIT does not have a solution for[188]. Unlike the computer industry where the source code for the programming is often either secret or undocumented, the Bible is different. GOD has documented everything in the Bible. HE does not wish you to be lost or confused. GOD wants you to use your devices (mind, body and spirit)[189] to its fullness.

Finally, don't be one of those Christians that live by the motto: *"When all else fails—read the directions."* I would like to remind you how costly that would be for you. The book of Hosea says, life is too expensive for that, *"My people are destroyed for lack of knowledge: because thou hast rejected knowledge, I will also reject thee, that thou shalt be no priest to me: seeing thou hast forgotten the law of thy GOD, I will also forget thy children."*[190]

The cost of a soul lost can never be measured; it is priceless. Please study! It allows you to be prepared at every moment for GOD's unmerited favor.

Works. The book of James is all about making sure our studying is supported by our works. Apostle James urges us to make sure our spiritual journey is experienced in action. While in the Waiting Room, you are being called to take as many practice flights as possible. Remember always that "faith without works is dead."[191] Your timely completion of homework assignments is essential for your journey.

---

[188] 1 Corinthians 10:13

[189] 3 John 2

[190] Hosea 4:6

[191] James 2:17

Chapter 15: Waiting Room

The Waiting Room is also the place where you get all that experience using the flight simulator. These simulation tests try your character, patience and perfect your faith. You obtain a significant amount of practice on what you should or should not do in the cockpit. How many times have you said to yourself that the next time that situation occurs you are going to respond differently? You can say that because real life has provided you enough experience in getting it wrong that you know the wrong answer by heart.

In order to respond correctly to flight simulation scenarios, you need the right answer. This will only occur when GOD's information is learned and applied, thereby creating a clean heart[192] in you. This transformation will allow you to know the right answer by heart–that is GOD's heart. HE has even provided you with your own personal coach (HOLY SPIRIT) who is already in your house 24/7 to insure that your complex device is working the way GOD intended it to, if you choose.

You will also practice the art of "Flybys" . This is where instead of engaging the enemy you respond like Nehemiah[193]. You observe and continue Flying.

The timely completion of GOD's homework assignments will be essential to your flight preparedness. The 24/7 personal coach (HOLY SPIRIT) is ready to provide instruction to anyone that has their mind in CHRIST.[194] The HOLY SPIRIT teaches you the thoughts and mind of GOD. Only the HOLY SPIRIT can reveal how the same particular passage in the Bible last year can mean something very different to you today.

In the Waiting Room, flight simulation training will be used to test and re-test your understanding of spiritual principles like faith, hope, perseverance, joy, patience and many others. Here, action

---

[192] Psalm 51:10

[193] Nehemiah 4

[194] 1 Corinthians 2:15-16

Fly With GOD

can be converted into wisdom and knowledge if you follow your coach's advice. GOD will provide you with all kinds of situations to test your application and knowledge of these spiritual flying concepts. Every time one simulation is passed, you will move on to the next one, until you're completely ready to Fly.

The COMFORTER will even teach you GOD's arithmetic—that one and one does NOT equal two. No, it is not addition or multiplication, but it is exponential! The power of GOD in action determines the amount of times your initial value will be raised by HIM!

HE will help you accomplish things like using two fish and five loaves of bread to feed more than 5,000 people;[195] and how to win without using one natural weapon.[196] If you want to really get out and stay out of the Waiting Room, I suggest that you immediately let your Coach help you.

Dear LORD,

Remind me I am the clay and YOU are the Potter. Give me the strength minute-by-minute to enjoy the place where I am right now. Please mold me and shape me in the most glorious ways.

Thank you In Jesus Name

Meditation Scriptures

- *Psalm 27:14 (KJV) Wait on the LORD: be of good courage, and HE shall strengthen thine heart: wait, I say, on the LORD.*

- *Psalm 40:1 (KJV) I waited patiently for the LORD; and HE inclined unto me, and heard my cry*

---

[195] Matthew 14:15-21

[196] 2 Chronicles 20

Chapter 15: Waiting Room

- James 2:18 (KJV) Yea, a man may say, Thou hast faith, and I have works: shew me thy faith without thy works, and I will shew thee my faith by my works.

What do you look like in the waiting room? Are you a glider, jumbo jet, or some vintage airplane that has only old stories to tell from the early days? Or Are you some toy plane fragile and full of flying fantasies? Whatever your type of aircraft, be encouraged, GOD offers all of us the ability to upgrade our aircraft to one of spiritual warfare. Review the aircraft types and features listed in the previous pages. Which do you most resemble or is it some other one?

Your Supernatural Features	
Awful Truth: Features desiring to change	**Awesome Truth:** Features we like and desire
1.	1.
2.	2.
3.	3.
4.	4.
5.	5.

Completion Date: ___/___/___

Part 5: Boarding

If you board the wrong train, it is no use running along the corridor in the other direction.

— Dietrich Bonhoeffer

Favor has just showed up

It is time to Board

The wait is over – it is time for you to report for "Duty".

Chapter 16: Reporting for Duty

REPORTING FOR DUTY: Engaging in GOD's course of action for your life.

The wait is over; it is time for you to report for "Duty" and board your plane. You're at the right gate, at the right time, and at the right place to depart. So, Ready—Set—Go! Go where? If you knew the exact pathway to where you were going, you would have left already. You would have never taken-up occupancy in the waiting room. The LORD knows how important time is to developing your gifts. You needed to learn the secret of waiting patiently. HE reminds you that "GOD's gifts and GOD's call are under full warranty—never canceled, never rescinded[197] whether it seems like a day or a thousand years on earth[198]." You just need to be ready for "Duty".

In the Book of Luke, the LORD tells you to occupy until HE comes[199]". Romans, Corinthians, and Ephesians encourage you to have your armor in place[200]. All of these references: duty, occupy, armor;

---

[197] Luke 19:13

[198] 2 Peter 3:8

[199] Luke 19:13

[200] Romans 13:12, 2 Corinthians 6:7, Ephesians 6:11, and Ephesians 6:13

Fly With GOD

clearly sound like battle talk to me. The armed forces will often mention terms like Reporting-for-Duty, battle-readiness, combat-ready and battle-efficiency. All of these terms relate to you – being prepared to take new territory for HIM.

You are ready for duty! The word "duty" is often defined as an assignment that is expected or required to do. Your view of the word will make all the difference in how you report for "duty" and where you are in the spiritual process of boarding your plane.

Will You Consider Your Duty a:

millstone?

calling?

charge?

chore?

commission?

commitment?

job?

load?

mission?

must?

need?

obligation?

occupation?

service?

undertaking?

work?

or finally a burden?

Chapter 16: Reporting For Duty

How ready you are to report for "duty" will determine how high you Fly. Ready to – give your reasonable sacrifice for the LORD[201] – your complete mind, body and soul. Ready to – reverence GOD and keep HIS commandments[202]. Ready to – proclaim and live the gospel of GOD[203].

Reporting for your assignment can be categorized in the following three (3) combat ways:

Absent Without Official Leave (AWOL) for Duty - very aware of GOD's voice, but while in the waiting room, you have somehow determined not to listen

Clarifying the Duty - willing, but not sure you heard correctly; need more information to be ready

Running for Duty - eagerly ready to begin the assignment

How you "Report for Duty" indicates where you are in the process of boarding your plane. Some people will exit the terminal during this processing stage for fear that they can't possibly accomplish the assignment GOD requires of them. Others may be tired, grumpy, unhappy, disillusioned, and possibly depressed; the trying of their faith did not produce patience. They may still be making deadlines, but there is no joy in their assignments.

Still others will be like these Noble Prize winners: President Jimmy Carter – taking action to facilitate peaceful solutions to international conflicts—from Haiti to North Korea; like Desmond Tutu – campaigning tirelessly against apartheid in South Africa; like Mother Teresa – bringing help to suffering humanity—particularly in the slums of Calcutta, India.

So how will you report for duty? Better yet, how have I?

---

[201]Romans 12:1

[202]Ecclesiastes 12:13

[203]Romans 15:16

Fly With GOD

> *I have on occasion rolled my wheels to the loading gate. I've had too many false starts to number. Years of sitting in the waiting room, then sitting on the tarmac only to be sent back to the waiting room. Yes, I have complained about being so tired! I was more than willing to be a hitchhiker on someone else's plane. I would be part of their team. I knew that I was not using all my gifts, but I wanted to Fly. Yes, I knew there would be problems in having to do it their way, but I was so confident that I could change them; and if not, it wouldn't be too bad would it? I was wrong—this isn't a team sport! No score—No partial credit! I wasted precious years not reporting for my own "Duty."*

Does any of this SELF-TALK sound familiar? When we settle for less than GOD's best we have grounded ourselves and chosen not to Fly. GOD's answer to hitching a ride is always NO!

> *Then, I had a better idea. I would become this workaholic, long hours and all nighters became my claim to fame. I was in a sprint, no marathon race for me. I would use my will power to run as fast as I could. I would do all GOD commanded on <u>my</u> accelerated schedule; and then relax. This didn't work for me either.*

If you reach this point in your journey, GOD might remind you, like HE did me, how when Caleb was 85 years old he declared he was stronger than he was in his youth and took the hardest territory[204]. Caleb knew the secret to the race, that it is a daily marathon with total commitment to GOD's goals[205]. Your desire to relax now based on the race you ran previously won't work for you either.

---

[204] Joshua 14

[205] Philippians 3:12-21

Chapter 16: Reporting For Duty

Or maybe you consider yourself so blessed that it is time to really enjoy those blessings and take a break. Didn't the prodigal son do that and received the fatted calf when he finished partying? Yes, that is true, but no one knows the time when their journey will be finished. That is why GOD reminds us of what happened to the five foolish virgins who had no oil in their lamps. When the bridegroom appeared, they were not ready, and the bridegroom left without them[206]. Leading us once more to the question of how will you report for "Duty"?

AWOL For Duty (Absent Without Official Leave). idual that knows what you have been called to do but refuse to go on Duty – AWOL? Both Jonah and King Saul are great biblical examples of this in action. They were men who were chosen for a special journey; journeys to positively affect the lives of thousands of individuals. Each chose to leave the airport terminal when initially presented with their assignment.

Jonah[207] story is told in Sunday schools all across the world. My nephews can tell you how Jonah didn't follow GOD's instructions. He ran away and was swallowed by a whale. I believe Jonah's pride led him away from his duty. His excuse was that if he told the people in Nineveh what the LORD said, they would repent. Then the LORD would not destroy them. Jonah was concerned about how that would make him look to the people. He had a reputation to maintain. The Good News is that Jonah takes only three days to come to his senses. His was temporarily AWOL. He finally follows GOD's call and the people of Nineveh repent and are not destroyed.

Now King Saul's story does not have a happy ending. His AWOL is permanent. The LORD told King Saul to go and utterly destroy the Amalekites. He was to fight against them until they and their

---

[206]Matthew 25:1-13

[207]Book of Jonah

Fly With GOD

possessions were utterly consumed. Nowhere in GOD's instructions to King Saul, did HE indicate that HE wanted anything left of the Amalekites. Unlike the people of Nineveh, GOD did not tell King Saul to warn the Amalekites. There is NO indication that they would ever be spared from annihilation. So when King Saul kept King Agag alive and sacrificed some of the spoils to the LORD, he was not following GOD's instructions[208]. King Saul's reason for not *"Reporting-for-Duty"* was that he feared the people. The Bad News is that King Saul never really repented. He continued to be AWOL. Eventually, King Saul was killed in battle and his kingdom was given to another.

Clarifying the Duty. There is a second group of individuals waiting to board the plane. They have progressed to the point that they are not really sure what they heard or if it was from GOD. They have questions. They want to report for duty, but are not sure how and when. Samuel, Hezekiah, Gideon and Ananias all had encounters that lead them to inquire further of GOD.

The prophet Samuel[209] is an excellent example of a righteous man desiring to report for duty. He is a very godly man. Samuel was dedicated to the service of GOD by his mother before he was even conceived. When GOD called Samuel to report for duty, he was lying down in the temple of the LORD. When the LORD called Samuel, he ran to his mentor—the prophet Eli and said, "Here I am; you called me." Eli answered "no". Samuel repeated that behavior again and again before Eli realized that the LORD must be calling Samuel. Eli helped Samuel 'Clarify his Duty' by instructing him on what to say to the LORD the next time HE called his name. Samuel heard from GOD. It was clarified and he reported for duty.

---

[208] 1 Samuel 15 and 31

[209] 1 Samuel 3

Chapter 16: Reporting For Duty

On the other hand, Gideon[210] used a fleece to make sure that GOD was calling him to battle the Midianites in order to save Israel. He was an obedient servant and the least qualified of his poor family. To clarify his duty, Gideon requested an event from GOD that would clearly defy the laws of nature. He initially requested a fleece of wool on the floor be made wet while the floor remains dry. GOD does just that. Gideon then requires more clarification for duty. He asked GOD not to be upset with him, but to do the opposite the next morning. GOD answers his request. After this final clarification, Gideon reports for duty.

Finally, I would like to mention Ananias[211] a devout Christian who was assigned the task to restore sight to the man whose occupation was to persecute Christians. Ananias is called to duty after Saul becomes blind on his way to Damascus. GOD instructs Ananias to find the man from Tarsus named Saul and place his hand on him to restore his sight. He seeks to clarify his duty by telling the LORD he has heard about this man's resume, which includes hurting and imprisoning Christians. The LORD clarifies Ananias's duty further by telling him that Saul is HIS chosen vessel to carry the Good News to the Gentiles. Ananias then reports for duty.

Running to Duty. The final group knows their assignments and is ready to Fly. They are like Isaiah and Nehemiah wanting to get started as soon as possible. When the LORD says, "Whom shall I send? And who will go for us?" Isaiah immediately says, "Here am I. Send me!" When Nehemiah receives the news that the wall around Jerusalem has still not been repaired, he solved a 70-year-old problem in 52 days[212]. I love GOD's math.

A spiritual journey grabbed him and would not let him go. Are you like Nehemiah, mulling over what you can do to effect a great

---

[210]Judges 6 and 7

[211]Act 9

[212]Nehemiah 6:15

Fly With GOD

change in the world? Have you fasted and mourned for days like he did? Or do you just feel unsettled in your spirit? If you have heard or seen a need—it is time for you to begin the process like Nehemiah. It Is Time For You To Act!

When you receive the news; sit down, pray, fast, weep and mourn over it if you have to. Remember, Nehemiah first moved through a repenting stage. He was very aware that sin and transgression can separate us from GOD's best in our life. So he made sure that did not happen to him—by seeking GOD's face and direction.

The 'Running for Duty' can be categorized in several ways: A desire to create something or do something that has never existed before; a desire to improve a situation; and finally a desire to repair a situation. These men ran for duty and mighty tasks were accomplished.

Not all desires to do well are the LORD's calls to duty. We must be careful to ensure our running for duty is under only GOD's direction. When King David desired to build the Temple for the LORD, it was a great desire but the LORD's response was "NO"[213]. GOD had not "called" him to duty for this task. When Martha was preparing food for JESUS and the others, she requested JESUS to tell her sister Mary to help, but JESUS' response was "NO."[214] GOD was not "calling" Mary to that duty. It is always important to make sure that, no matter how godly the task seems, it is only godly if the LORD has called you to this duty. Otherwise you're AWOL.

When You Are At The Wrong Duty Station

– Your Work Is Left Undone –

Some pilots from the Bible who did something that had never been done before were Noah, Solomon, Mary and Peter.

---

[213] 1 Chronicles 22:5-19
[214] Luke 10:39-42

Chapter 16: Reporting For Duty

Noah built the Ark

Solomon built the Temple

Mary carried, birthed and nurtured the SAVIOR

Peter walked on water

GOD called them to duty and they went eagerly – **Changing the World**.

You may be called to duty to improve a situation, like Samuel. Samuel was called by GOD to anoint David to replace King Saul (Israel's first king). King Saul was a disobedient leader. Samuel didn't fix the situation because GOD never desired for the Hebrew children to have a king in the first place. He was able to improve the Hebrews' destiny by anointing a man that had an obedient spirit.

For my final examples of being called to duty to repair a situation, I will use Nehemiah and JESUS. Nehemiah repaired the wall around the Temple in Jerusalem, while JESUS tore the veil of the Temple from top to bottom to repair the damage Adam and Eve did in the Garden of Eden. JESUS repaired the breech which enables us to regain the relationship humankind had with the LORD in Eden. Each repairing the Temple allowing GOD's people to dwell; one physically and the other spiritually[215].

LORD—Thank you for calling and lifting me up. Every step I make under YOUR direction is important to YOUR Kingdom. Please give me power and strength to continuously follow YOUR orders with zeal.

In JESUS name – Amen

---

[215] 2 Corinthians 6:16

Fly With GOD

Meditation Scriptures

- Luke 11:33 (KJV) No man, when he hath lighted a candle, putteth it in a secret place, neither under a bushel, but on a candlestick, that they which come in may see the light.

- 1 Corinthians 2:9 (KJV) ...Eye hath not seen, nor ear heard, neither have entered into the heart of man, the things which GOD hath prepared for them that love him.

- Psalm 119:105 (KJV) Thy Word is a lamp unto my feet, and a light unto my path.

Where Do You Stand On "Reporting For Duty"? Running, Clarifying, or Absent Without Official Leave (AWOL). GOD often gives us numerous duty assignments, some for family, others for friends, and still others for our work. How are you following them?

Your Truth Time	
Awful: AWOL	**Awesome: Clarifying or Running**
What is GOD saying	What is GOD saying
What are you doing	What are you doing

Completion Date: ___/ ___/ ____

Chapter 17: Manifest

MANIFEST: A List Of Passengers Carried On Your Plane

So if you're reporting for duty, you have just one more boarding detail to accomplish as the pilot for your journey, the Manifest. As pilot, you are required to review the list of passengers occupying seats on your plane. Time to check the plane's Manifest. The Manifest is divided into three (3) categories: Cockpit Crew, Flight Attendants, and Passengers. You determine which categories will be filled and the occupants. The more empty seats in the passenger section, the smoother the ride and the faster you will arrive at your next destination.

Cockpit Crew. The cockpit is reserved for the pilot team: you, the HOLY SPIRIT, JESUS, and GOD. This section of the aircraft has been designed to safely guide you to your proper destination. It has a sophisticated autopilot system that can conquer any internal or external situations. The system is capable of maneuvering in all types of weather conditions and providing safe lift-off and landing.

The autopilot system is extremely sensitive to internal conditions in the cockpit. It is only engaged when you surrender to the other pilots (HOLY SPIRIT, JESUS, and GOD). At anytime you are out of alignment with your approved course, the navigation mechanism

Fly With GOD

immediately changes to the manual mode. The manual mode is very cumbersome; just one wrong move and the aircraft quickly spins out of control.

If it is not evident yet, there is a weak link in the cockpit and that weak link is you. The good news is that CHRIST's strength prevails in our weakness[216]. The autopilot is just moments away from being engaged when you call on JESUS[217] just like Peter did when he walked on the water.

Flight Attendants. The flight attendants' section of the aircraft is reserved to assist you in gaining altitude on your journey. The attendants are individuals GOD sends alongside of you to help you with your mission. These attendants may be involved in your life for a moment, a season or a lifetime. During this time, they are being guided by the LORD to support your flight's speed and height.

Flight attendants have played a vital role in the Bible. When Moses was sent by GOD back to Egypt to lead the Children of Israel to the Promised Land, he was sent with Aaron as his flight attendant to assist him in his journey. When Esther was sent to King Ahasuerus' palace to prepare to be his queen and save her people, she was sent with her uncle Mordecai as her flight attendant to stay close by and to assist her in her journey. When Mary was found pregnant with our savior JESUS CHRIST, she was sent with her fiancé Joseph as her flight attendant. He knowingly married and supported the birth and nurturing of JESUS CHRIST. These flight attendants led by GOD, clearly assisted their pilots in gaining spiritual altitude.

Then there is my favorite flight attendant, Jonathan (King Saul's son), he pledged his life, his crown, and his descendants to David[218]. The Bible declares that Jonathan loved David and their souls were knit together becoming one in the spirit. Jonathan showed respect

---

[216] 2 Corinthians 12:9-11

[217] Matthew 14:27-32

[218] 1 Samuel 18-20, 2 Samuel 1, 9

Chapter 17: Manifest

to his father, but still followed the LORD by faithfully protecting David from his father's attempts to kill him.

Not all flight attendants have to be believers. GOD has a way of providing you favor wherever HE leads you. These flight attendants are used by GOD in a supernatural way to assist you in your journey. They may say things like "I never did this before," "I can't put my finger on it," or "I just feel good about you."

Time after time we may find ourselves the recipients of this kind of assistance. Daniel understood it well as he experienced this type of assistance throughout his journey. It started with the guard in Nebuchadnezzar's court and continued through several kings' reigns[219]. Joseph experienced similar favor. His started with his father showing him favoritism by making him a coat, then in Potiphar's house, in prison and finally by Pharaoh – the King of Egypt. Wherever Joseph went, GOD found a way to send a flight attendant to help him[220].

Then there is the power of a joint vision. This is when we find ourselves going exactly to the same destination and our gifts complement each other. Paul and Silas had a joint vision—their relationship[221] was so strong that prison couldn't keep them captive. In The Book of Acts, they are found praying and singing praises at the midnight hour. That joint vision in action caused a miraculous earthquake to break their chains, opening their doors, and finally converting their jailer to Christianity.

Finally, when choosing a flight attendant remember what GOD told Samuel when he saw David's brother – Eliab. *"Looks aren't everything. Don't be impressed with his looks and stature. I've already*

---

[219] Book of Daniel

[220] Genesis 37 - 41

[221] Acts 16:25-39

eliminated him. GOD judges persons differently than humans do. Men and women look at the face; GOD looks into the heart[222]."

Being able to benefit spiritually from the flight attendants we choose, requires that we connect with the right people on our journey. Flight attendants must be selected very carefully if you want to fly high.

Paul chose Silas to fly with him because he had seen his character in action (faithfulness, loyalty, love of GOD, obedience, and more) and that proved to be a successful journey. On the other hand, Sarah who thought she saw some of those same characteristics in her handmaiden chose Hagar to fly with her. Once Hagar became pregnant –she proved to be a horrible flight attendant looking down on her mistress.

Not all of your choices for flight attendants will work, but as soon as their character reveals a critical flaw, it is time for you to relieve them of duty.

---

[222] 1 Samuel 16:7 MSG

Chapter 17: Manifest

Who are your current Flight Attendants? Are they helping you? What particular aspect of your journey are they supporting you in?

Your Current Flight Attendants		
Names	**Strengths**	**Weaknesses**

Completion Date: ___/___/___

Flight Attendant Assessment. Take some time to pray about the names you listed on the previous page. Does your page reflect the names of individuals that are really helpful to your journey? Or are there a few that should not be considered flight attendants?

Flight attendants are part of your inner circle. They often enjoy complete access to your mission. You may now need to consider changing the status of some of your flight attendants to insure you receive the assistance you need for your journey. Remember you're the pilot, this is your flight Manifest, you are responsible for doing your part to insure lift and altitude is sustained.

Flight Attendant Recruitment. Did you review the list of flight attendants and realize you don't have enough attendants? You are probably not alone. When I first realized why I was unable to maintain altitude, I had to look at the quality of my flight attendants. I had not sought out the best flight attendants. Since then, I have not only prayed for the ability to discern spirits, but the courage to act on what GOD has shown me regarding potential attendants. It is amazing what GOD will reveal when you ask. I started watching to see if these potential flight attendants were faithful over the little things. Each day, I'm learning how to better screen and add to my flight Manifest.

Flight Attendant Retention. Your flight attendant list represents people that give to you; in order for you to retain them the giving must be mutual. Giving keeps those Flight Attending blessings flowing. When GOD tells you to give, you must be willing to give—even if it seems to jeopardize your livelihood. For example, this means in order to have a Jonathan spirit in your life, you must be willing to have a David spirit in you. David and Jonathan kept their promises.

In this example, we see that GOD does want us to pour into what HE has determined to be part of his royal priesthood. Jonathan was not pouring into an ordinary man. David really loved GOD and was able to share HIS love with his friend—Jonathan. Even

Chapter 17: Manifest

death did not separate David's commitment to give to his worthy flight attendant. David kept his vow by blessing Jonathan's heir. He found Jonathan's son Mephibosheth and treated him as if he were his own son. Their flight attendant relationship went on to the next generation[223].

Passengers. This section is reserved for passengers. This area of the plane will include people that will hinder or impede your progress in the air. They will hold on to your wings. These are people I classify as neutral, stowaways, terrorists, murderers, saboteurs, naysayers, and mercenaries. Their mission whether intentionally or unintentionally is to delay or stop your vision, for a moment, season or a lifetime. They often try to hitch a ride under the guise of being a flight attendant but along the journey they show their motives and true character. They should be neutralized immediately, ejected from the plane even if it is in mid-air.

King Saul would be considered an attempted murderer. He started out as a flight attendant to David but quickly changed to a passenger who plots to murder him. In the beginning of their relationship, King Saul makes David one of his beloved armor-bearers because he is so pleased with how David's harp abilities have helped him feel better and forced the evil spirit to leave him[224]. Next thing we know, King Saul is so ridden with jealousy over David's victories in battle and people's praise—he is trying to have David killed. To neutralize this passenger, David spent many years fleeing from King Saul's presence.

Then there is the example of the mercenary effect on the prophet[225] from Judah. This prophet has personally received a Word from the LORD instructing him not to go backwards in his journey, or eat bread or drink water. He first shows up in the Bible telling

---

[223] 2 Samuel 9:6-10

[224] 1 Samuel 16

[225] 1 Kings 13

Fly With GOD

King Jeroboam about a disaster that will befall his kingdom. This prophet is so anointed that when the king tries to grab him, the king's hand shrivels up. The king comes to his senses and asks that same prophet to intercede on his behalf—the hand is then healed.

The prophet later in his journey meets a mercenary passenger (another prophet). He listens to this mercenary which countermands his orders from the LORD. He believes the passenger instead of what he personally heard from GOD. A lion kills the prophet upon leaving the mercenary's home. Taking this passenger onboard cost this prophet from Judah his life.

This story is very important to your journey because it reveals how a man of GOD (also a prophet) can deceive you for their own personal gain. I believe this Passenger's motives was greed. He wanted to get a piece of what this man had. He wanted some of his anointing and blessings. This serves as a warning about the dangers of putting any instruction above the LORD, no matter who says it—pastor, prophet, parent or significant other. GOD clearly says every time you go back against HIS wishes the vision HE has given you is in jeopardy of dying either in whole or in part. Taking on these passengers can cause spiritual death. Your dreams and purposes are all placed in danger.

Some of us may have received grace and/or mercy allowing our loss of altitude not to cause us to crash. We have been given another chance to move in the vision GOD has for us. But others will die without having reached their destination because the passengers they have on their Manifest.

I can't emphasize enough that the mercenary was a religious leader. GOD wants us to try[226] every spirit to make sure they are not false. By all religious evidence, it should have been wonderful to fellowship with another Christian. The Bible even mentions how

---

[226] 1 John 4:1

Chapter 17: Manifest

wonderful it is to fellowship with our sisters and brothers[227], but it is only wonderful, if GOD says it to you. In the New Testament, we are warned about [228]false prophets — that they shall deceive the very elect. I believe these passages were truly written for the mature Christian to strengthen their often solitary walk with the LORD. To not allow other Christians, no matter how devoted they seem, to interfere with GOD's Word for your life.

Not everyone you start with might understand where GOD is taking you. Sometimes the elder statesman may impede your spiritual progress. As you develop your spiritual discernment skills it will be easier for you to spot a passenger. You will be able to identify the ones posing as flight attendants. Eventually you will create your own "No-Fly" list. The names will include certain folks and/or certain discernable spirits that you know NO MATTER WHAT, <u>not</u> to let in your plane.

Flight Attendant or Passenger. Earlier, I focused solely on "one-way-relationships". You'll notice that King Saul was a Passenger to David, but as you may recall David was a flight attendant to King Saul. I mention this example because there may be times when GOD will call you to be a flight attendant to someone who is your passenger. This can only be accomplished with GOD's wisdom.

Dear LORD,

Please continue to give me knowledge and wisdom in all my relationships. Increase my ability to discern advocates from foes; and the courage to act godly with this knowledge.

In JESUS name – Amen

---

[227]Acts 2:42

[228]Matthew 24:24

Meditation Scriptures

- *Proverbs 18:24 (KJV) A man that hath friends must shew himself friendly: and there is a friend that sticketh closer than a brother.*

- *1 John 4 (KJV) Beloved, believe not every spirit, but try the spirits whether they are of God: because many false prophets are gone out into the world.*

Chapter 17: Manifest

*Who Is On Your **No-Fly** List?*

Passengers	
Names	**Discernable Spirits**
	A) B) C)
	A) B) C)
	A) B) C)
	A) B) C)
	A) B) C)
	A) B) C)
	A) B) C)
	A) B) C)

Completion Date: ___/____/____

Part 6: Take-off

He who loves, flies, runs, and rejoices; he is free and nothing holds him back.

— Henri Matisse

YOUR CREW IS READY – WHERE IS THE PLANE?

During the check-in and boarding phase your take-off was determined by waiting room behavior, passenger manifest, baggage and spiritual maturity. As you rely more and more on the will of GOD your take-off is guaranteed.

Chapter 18: Flight Plan

FLIGHT PLAN: GOD's route for your life. A plan which takes into account the flight plans of the entire world.

Be Prepared to Fly

Be Prepared to Succeed! With the complete revelation and knowledge that it is time to Fly, millions of Christians will suddenly suffer from fear of flying. They are actually afraid that GOD has asked them to do something that will cause them to crash and burn.

I believe Esther felt that same way for a moment, when she reminded Mordecai of her possible death if she approached the King uninvited[229]. But Mordecai's response was to remind her that she was prepared to Fly. He told Esther *"...who knoweth whether thou art come to the kingdom for such a time as this?"* Much like her, GOD has a plan for you. You are more prepared then you will ever know because GOD has your Flight Plan.

The previous chapters emphasized the fact that as a Christian, GOD has a travel itinerary with your name on it. JESUS never intended HIS followers to stay in the crawl, walk, or even in the run mode.

---

[229] Esther 4

Fly With GOD

These modes were to be used to prepare you to Fly. GOD desires you to become mature and fearless in your spiritual journeys.

You are to Fly from one destination to the next; not by economy or public transportation, but in your own private aircraft. Every surrendered Christian is being groomed for the pilot seat along with first class accommodation to every destination. So just like Esther, GOD has designed a plan for you to Fly. You must do your part to ensure you are completely prepared.

> *Did GOD give you all the details for your Flight Plan when you were packing or is HE still releasing them?*

GOD promises to be patient providing you the time required to prepare your Flight Plan. HE reminds us in Peter that *"one day is with the LORD as a thousand years, and a thousand years as one day*[230].*"* But the pivotal point of this verse is "with the LORD." This means in the company of the LORD. That means we have to stay in HIS presence. No gaps in time or space in our relationship or adjustments to our assignments. The "with the LORD" is not measured cumulatively but continuously.

This may possibly be the reason why our Flight Plans are at different points of completion. The Bible is full of stories of individuals who were provided their Flight Plan in various ways.

Isaiah and Noah's Flight Plan experience happened in one day. As you may recall, the prophet Isaiah was taken to the LORD's throne where he was given his commission[231]. At that point, he had a face-to-face encounter with the LORD where he displayed his repentant heart and was cleansed of his sins and given details of his Flight Plan along with the implementation timetable. Noah, when he was building the ark was given a very detailed Flight Plan to build the ark. GOD specified the type of wood, how the wood would be

---

[230] 2 Peter 3:8-9

[231] Isaiah 6

Chapter 18: Flight Plan

treated, the dimensions; location of the door, the number of decks, when to go in and who would occupy the ark.

Most of us will not have that experience, your Flight Plans may seem more like a 1,000 years. If you are like me, your Flight Plan has been unfolding as you walked with the LORD. Much like Moses, you will be making real-time adjustments as you received the data. He was given the last line of the Flight Plan during his first encounter with GOD at the burning bush.

GOD sent him to Pharaoh to bring the children of Israel out of Egypt to a land of milk and honey, "the Promised Land." Moses is told that Pharaoh will not want to let them go, GOD will have to hurt Pharaoh in order for him to release them; and when they are released, they will leave with wealth from the Egyptians. This was only the destination "the Promised Land", the rest of the Flight Plan is completed during his 40 years in the desert.

Moses' close relationship with GOD did not exempt him from having to wait for his Flight Plan to unfold. At one point in his journey, even Moses felt the need to request GOD to let him in on HIS plans for the people[232]. But GOD responds by saying *"My presence shall go with thee, and I will give thee rest[233]."* Modern day translation is *"As you go with GOD – You will know[234]."* Clearly, GOD is sovereign and will provide the flight details when HE chooses to regardless of how close your relationship. HE sees your mission completed; HE promises you victory if you wait for HIS Flight Plan.

Moses' Flight Plan was not determined by the shortest distance between Egypt and "the Promised Land", but his travelers' mindsets. Theologians have estimated that had the journey been about the distance, they would have arrived at their destination in less than a month. But the details of Moses' Flight Plan were

---

[232] Exodus 33:12-17

[233] Exodus 33:14

[234] Lily emphasis

Fly With GOD

determined by the people he was to lead to "the Promised Land". His Flight Plan was about changing the hearts and minds of his fellow travelers which required decades to accomplish. GOD's Flight Plan for delivering the "Children of Israel" to "the Promise Land" took Moses over 40 years to complete and only at his death were the people ready to enter into their promise.

Not every Flight Plan which unfolds as we go will take 40 years. Thank GOD many are much shorter. Take Nehemiah, for instance, he is best known for accomplishing a task that was left undone for over 70 years in just 52 days[235]. This man took his grief and sorrow about the destruction of the walls of Jerusalem and received a Flight Plan. This plan catapulted him into divine action in the fraction of the time it took Moses.

Nehemiah's journey provides a wonderful framework for the process of positioning yourself for receiving the details for your Flight Plan[236]. Here you discover the specifics on how he was able to hear from GOD. He asked in prayer. The New Testament further supports Nehemiah's actions by saying, *"Be careful for nothing; but in every thing by prayer and supplication with thanksgiving let your requests be made known unto GOD[237]."* Making his requests specifically known to GOD is exactly what Nehemiah did.

Nehemiah grieved and mourned over the condition of Jerusalem's walls and gates. He then enters into a period of worship and praise to GOD. This is when Nehemiah reminds GOD of HIS covenant with Moses regarding Israel's repentance. Which is: "if Israel is faithful to GOD, GOD will gather all which were scattered to a place marked with GOD's name."

Nehemiah tells GOD, he is part of that group that repented. He then asked GOD to hear his prayer and make him successful. After

---

[235]Nehemiah 1; 6:15

[236]Nehemiah 1:5-11

[237]Philippians 4:6

Chapter 18: Flight Plan

repenting, fasting, and praying, Nehemiah receives his Flight Plan, receiving the favor he needed from King Artaxerxes to accomplish the mission.

Here we witness firsthand, expect answers to prayer when they hinge on the promises of GOD. As we prepare our Flight Plan for lift-off we must remember, GOD will keep HIS Word, it does not matter how long ago HE said it. The plans can be detailed or general but GOD will do it. The Bible is filled with Flight Plans that initially had only a beginning and an end. What occupied the middle for these men and women's Flight Plans was their faith and hope in the promise GOD had given them.

This kind of faith and hope for some of us will never be developed if GOD first gave us all the Flight Plan details. GOD says the routes to these attributes are developed on your journey through trials and tribulations[238]. To Fly, your faith must be strong enough to supernaturally see your assignments finished even when it seems the promise has tarried. Only then can you see GOD's plan as it unfolds and execute each task. So whether the Flight Plan is a paragraph long or a detailed outline only when GOD approves it, are you ready to go!

An approved Flight Plan is required, remember many are called but few are chosen[239]. The tarmac is littered with millions of planes, but few are directly and constantly communicating with GOD for their lift-off. The pilots in these grounded planes do not have an approved Flight Plan. Some pilots have received the call, but remain on the tarmac without an up-to-date Flight Plan from GOD.

Habakkuk reminds you to watch and then make plain what you receive, even if it seems to take a while, it is not late[240]. The items may have to be refined and refined again as your Flight Plan is

---

[238] Romans 5:1-5

[239] Matthew 20:16

[240] Habakkuk 2:3

Fly With GOD

revealed. These changes allow you to flow in the Holy Spirit while enabling you to experience GOD's perfect peace with every new situation.

It is always important to count the cost of your decisions before you make them. Are they GOD driven? Have you made lesser choices to eliminate stress and/or cause momentary happiness, but in the end hampered your ability to be in GOD's presence.

When GOD provides you with new information for your Flight Plan, you must have the ability to adapt your Flight Plan to HIS way of doing things. You must immediately change your priorities in order to keep GOD's best on the top of your Flight Plan.

There will be some Christians unable to adapt to this way of living. They will experience the need to control all aspects of their Flight Plan. They will become suddenly overly concerned about every detail of their trip. They will want to know where they're going; why they're going there and what will happen once they get there. The sheer thought of enjoying their journey is out of the question for them. If they want to Fly they will eventually have to release their control.

GOD will always provide you with enough information on your Flight Plan for lift-off. The Bible is full of stories in both the Old and New Testaments of men and women just like you who after the initial call had to daily adapt their Flight Plan. They understood what was meant when the Psalmist said, *"Thy Word is a lamp unto my feet, and a light unto my path. I have sworn, and I will perform it, ...*[241]*."* He knew there would always be enough light, or in your case enough data for your Flight Plan.

There may even be adjustments that occur while airborne; things that are added or are taken off your Flight Plan. GOD's message to you about your Flight Plan is the same one HE gave to Habakkuk

---

[241] Psalm 119:105-106

Chapter 18: Flight Plan

after he wrote the vision. HE told him that the *"just shall live by faith[242];"* HE has and will provide. Your faith will enable you to recognize, follow and enjoy GOD's Flight Plan for your journeys.

Dear LORD,

Allow me to stay on course. Let my will line up with YOUR plans for me. Remind me that darkness allows me to clearly focus on YOUR light.

In JESUS CHRIST – Amen

Meditation Scriptures

- *James 1:22-24 (KJV) But be ye doers of the Word, and not hearers only, deceiving your own selves. For if any be a hearer of the Word, and not a doer, he is like unto a man beholding his natural face in a glass: For he beholdeth himself, and goeth his way, and straightway forgetteth what manner of man he was.*

- *1 Corinthians 13:11-13 (KJV) When I was a child, I spake as a child, I understood as a child, I thought as a child: but when I became a man, I put away childish things. For now we see through a glass, darkly; but then face to face: now I know in part; but then shall I know even as also I am known.*

---

[242]Habakkuk 2:3-4

Fly With GOD

You have read over 70% of this book, so what has changed? In "Your Truth Time", write as much as you can, this is only a snapshot—GOD will reveal much more at your appointed[243] time.

Your Truth Time (complete each section, use more paper if necessary)	
Awful	**Awesome**
People	People
Place	Place
Things	Things

**Completion Date: ___/___/___ - 4th Time

** You will see this form again, each time adding or subtracting information based on revelation and knowledge from the LORD. Be sure to date your entries so that you can chart your progress.

---

[243] Habakkuk 2:3

Chapter 19: Fuel

FUEL: The physical resources needed to power your flight.

Fuel can be the money, equipment, materials, and/or labor you will or might use to support your journeys. The amount, type and quality of Fuel are important to your lift-off. All of these factors play a critical role in your journey. Just like in the natural – if your tank is empty or you have the wrong type of gas or quality, you may not achieve lift-off, or worse crash your plane. The spiritual realm works the same way. You require GOD's Fuel in your tank.

Obtaining the right Fuel has challenged the people of GOD throughout the ages. The Ancients' questions were not unlike the ones Christians pose today. Questions like: Where can I obtain resources? Who will help me? How will I eat? Where will I find shelter? **Now the real question is ...** how many times have you personally had the same thoughts?

What you have to realize is a little of the right Fuel is all you need with GOD to change a crisis into a victory. You have to understand that in the spiritual realm there is a huge difference between being empty and almost empty. Almost empty never matters, when what is left in your tank is GOD's highest grade of Fuel. Just a smidgen of

Fly With GOD

this superpower Fuel will produce the best lift and flight sustainability you can possibly imagine.

Just like in the natural – the supernatural Fuel ranges from low to high grade. The highest grade of Fuel is often created when we have what appears to be our least amount of resources. Those times when you can truthfully say, "I have hardly anything!" That little bit in the MASTER's hands can move your tank from almost EMPTY to supernaturally FULL in an instant.

Where are you? EMPTY or FULL? And what do you have?). Even when you think you are empty – you are not! An anointed person can look at you and see something very different. They can see what is very precious on the inside of you.

When the prophet Elisha[244] was approached by the widow of one of his former prophets, he saw precious "Fuel" that could save her, her sons, and allow them to live. Elisha asked the woman, what she had in her house. Her response was "nothing," and then, she seemed to remember something that she obviously viewed as inconsequential. She then says "except a little oil." She has Fuel, let me restate the matter, she has SUPERCHARGED FUEL! Nothing is inconsequential with GOD, nothing is by accident, and every molecule has a purpose in your tank.

With that bit as her Fuel, Elisha was able to instruct her to borrow as many empty jars from her neighbors as she could; to go home and lock the doors behind her and her sons; and to fill those jars. When they follow Elisha's commands they are able to take that little bit of oil and fill up every jar in her house, before the oil stopped.

They went from being almost empty to supernaturally full by using what they had. The little Fuel this widow had, became the seed that financed her and her family's future. Elisha's final command

---

[244] 2 Kings 4

Chapter 19: Fuel

to the widow was: to sell the oil; pay off her debts; and to live on the rest. So that means, the little bit of Fuel saved her two sons from slavery which was her initial request. Furthermore, it gave them additional resources to live – taking care of her future which she never requested, but I'm sure she desired.

Elisha reveals two important principles to Fueling your plane; they are recognizing seed and finding its purpose. Others in the Bible seemed to have understood how these principles lead to abundant breakthroughs. When, the disciples told JESUS to send the crowd away because they had nothing to eat; HE asked the disciples, "How much food do you have?"[245] JESUS used five loaves to feed five thousand people, and seven loaves to feed four thousand people, and still had leftovers. Then there was Elijah, when the woman from Zarephath told him she had only enough meal and oil for a last supper with her son. He asked her to use the handful of meal in a barrel, and a little oil to feed three people day-after-day until it rained. These are both examples of how GOD used meager amounts of Fuel to fill tanks for HIS purpose.

The first thing JESUS, Elisha, and Elijah did was to check the gas tank gauge. They got the facts from the disciples, the widow, and the woman from Zarephath. Then they got the truth from GOD. This process will always begin with GOD opening eyes to see what HE sees, a full tank of Fuel for a divine purpose.

The first time, I heard these passages preached – it haunted me. It continues to haunt me because it forces me to constantly ask and answer the hard questions. Questions like: What gift? What talent? What anointing? What power has GOD given me to get wealth?[246] What have I over looked? Why did I run to the left and to the right looking for someone to help me, when I had it all the time? Thus the question you should ask yourself is what do

---

[245]Mark 8:1-21

[246]Deuteronomy 8:18

Fly With GOD

you have at home or should I say in your temple? What's your gas gauge on?

Think about what you have? The answer might be you don't have, but a little. When you think you have nothing at all that can lead you to your "Refueling" moment. Even a little bit that you have can cause your tank to be full and for you to Fly. You can have enough to pay off your debts, set the captives free, create something wonderful, and of course enough to really soar high.

GOD intends to bless the Fuel that HE has already deposited in you. But having the Fuel is not enough if you are unable to recognize it. You must spend time with the Fuel GIVER in order to recognize your Fuel. Then you have to follow HIS commands. This widow woman went home, locked her door, and obeyed. Are you ready to do the same?

Once you get your Word, you need to stop constantly searching for external support, instead close yourself off long enough for prayer and meditation to bless you. Similar to the experience of the widow pouring oil into those vessels, GOD can pour into your earthly vessel more than enough to bless you, your family and the world. That is why it is critical for you to take the time to look into your temple and figure out with GOD's guidance what Fuel you have right now that can be used for your flight.

Using your GOD given resources the way GOD intended them to be used allows you to Fly. Knowing what is inside of you will help you understand what you thought was nothing is Fuel for your journey. GOD has been waiting for you to recognize HIS miraculous power.

You need to understand what HE placed in you at the beginning of time. This Fuel can ensure that your needs and desires are met at the appointed time. The "Awesome Truth" is you are never lacking for anything. All you need for this day HE has promised to give

Chapter 19: Fuel

you[247]. But what you really need is an intimate relationship with the GIVER in order to recognize the seed and allow it to fill your empty tank.

It often takes someone outside of us, a spiritual leader, a friend, a stranger, or perhaps even the rocks to cry out; to remind us how to recognize seed. When the Spirit of GOD whispers in your ears with a still small voice[248], it is just to remind you that the Fuel supply (GOD, HOLY SPIRIT, and JESUS) was there all the time. GOD is calling you to find out what you have in your home, or should I say, temple today.

What's in Your Temple?

You have all you need right now. You don't have to venture out, you don't have to steal, cheat or copy someone else, just be you. You are fearfully and wonderfully made by GOD[249].

You are blessed beyond measure. Blessed enough, not only to pay off your debts, but to live; and the "live," GOD uses here, is to live more abundantly[250]. To move into a dimension that you have never moved into before; to be worry free, to not be concerned about anything[251].

Remember, even in your physical poverty, you always have something valuable; right where you are; there is a creative idea, there is something. If you are willing to search your heart, you will find it. From the beginning of time, GOD placed something of extreme value in you, for such a time as this.

---

[247]Psalm 68:19

[248]1 Kings 19:11-13

[249]Psalm 139:14

[250]Eph 3:20

[251]Matthew 6

Fly With GOD

Own Fuel. The Fuel must be your own. It must come from inside of you. That is why it is so important that you consistently seclude yourself with GOD for refueling. Make sure GOD has called you to Fly in your current direction. You need to make sure you are not taking on the Flight Plan of a friend or family member, but, the Flight Plan which is genuinely yours. If it is HIS plan, then be confident that HE has provided the Fuel.

Let me help you understand the importance of this ownership principle. Would a farmer plant crops on land he did not own or have any rights to? NO, that's CRAZY— right? He would know that if he planted on someone else's land, at harvest time the fruit would not be his, but theirs. That is why it is important to plant on soil that is already on your property. In your case, it is important to take what is in your temple and improve on it.

When King David desired to build the Temple[252] for the LORD, it seemed like an anointed idea, but the LORD's response was "NO". GOD had not given David that territory. On the other hand, when Nehemiah went to re-build the wall around the temple, it was GOD's vision for him, so GOD blessed him with Fuel. Too often we want to build on property that we don't even own. GOD has not given us that territory. It's someone else's "Flight Plan". You need to work on whatever GOD has already declared as yours.

There is No Gas Crisis. You must resist using lack of money as your excuse and just Fly. It doesn't matter if your lack of Fuel was caused by poor stewardship or outside factors. There is no gas crisis with GOD. The seeming lack of Fuel can't stop you from flying when GOD says you are ready to take-off.

When it was time for Gideon to take-off, GOD sent him an angel to respond to his concerns about his assignment and lack of Fuel. The angel tells him the LORD is with him and calls him a mighty

---

[252] 1 Chronicles 22:5-19

Chapter 19: Fuel

man of valor. Why? because GOD's plan for him is to save Israel from the Midianites.

Gideon's response to the angel is to question the truth of the angel's statement. He proceeds to tell him how they have suffered, with no sign of the miracles which their fathers had told them about. The angel has to repeat the directive, to which Gideon reminds the angel that his family is poor, and he is the least in his father's house.[253] All of this, GOD knew, Gideon was part of GOD's plan. HE called him by name. Finally, Gideon fills up his tank. He fastens his spiritual seatbelt and takes flight – soaring into victory.

Have you ever heard of the Bishop Boys? By all accounts they lacked both financial and technical Fuel. They were two sons of a very devout Bishop in a United Brethren Church in Dayton, Ohio. You may know them as Orville and Wilbur Wright, The Wright Brothers. But what you may not know is the highly funded folks did not produce the first flight, but the barely financed and self-taught Wright Brothers did.

What would you think if you heard about a 33 year old single man, who had never been to college, worked at a bicycle shop and was still living with his brothers, sisters and parents? Would you think failure or success? The Wright Brothers' first trip to Kitty Hawk took place when they were both over 30 years old. They made a decision while still living with daddy to fill up their tanks. The Wright Brothers, with their limited resources, eventually became one of the most successful teams in American history.

The Wright Brothers' story, more than any other in modern history, displays the gap between who you were, and who you can be, if you choose to Fly. The Fuel that is in you cannot be measured. What the world could never get over was how these ordinary men in a bicycle shop in Dayton Ohio, could believe, could conceive, and achieve, first flight. What the world needs to be reminded of

---

[253] Judges 6

Fly With GOD

again, in you, is that GOD can and will if you let HIM take your creativity and ability, and make something wonderful out of almost nothing. GOD is in the business of taking empty Fuel tanks and making them full. HE is the GOD All Sufficient, the GOD of More Than Enough, HE is El Shaddai!

GOD tells us I am EL SHADDAI, the "GOD Almighty—GOD All Sufficient", the one that can supply more than you need. I believe that when Elisha spoke into the life of the woman who was afraid her sons would be sold into slavery[254], it wasn't the aspect of Jehovah Jireh that he called on, because that would have only provided enough Fuel for today, but instead Elisha must have called on El Shaddai the "All Sufficient GOD" which touches not only today, but our future.

Finally, if you are one of those Christians that feel your tank is empty because you don't have the financial resources to Fly, it is time to get full. It is time to press into the *"More Than Enough GOD."* The GOD, that if HE gave you the vision, HE will give you more than enough to bring it to pass. The GOD that took five loaves of bread to feed 5,000 with leftovers. This same GOD can take one dollar, place six zeros after it and make it a million – in an instant.

Dear LORD,

Thank you for allowing me to really live in this new dimension in YOUR assigned territory. My prayer right now is that YOU would allow my eyes to be open to see the divine resources YOU have given.

Let me know what I need to spend time on and reflect on, so that it becomes bigger than I ever thought; also show me how to use YOUR blessings to diligently serve YOU and others as YOU so direct.

---

[254] 2 Kings 4

LORD, please bless whatever is in me that YOU deem precious, expand it so that I may live more abundantly the rest of my life. Let me move to a place where blessings over take blessings. Most of all allow me to share this truth with others.

In JESUS' name, I pray.

Meditation Scriptures

- *Mark 4:31-32 (KJV) It is like a grain of mustard seed, which, when it is sown in the earth, is less than all the seeds that be in the earth: But when it is sown, it groweth up, and becometh greater than all herbs, and shooteth out great branches; so that the fowls of the air may lodge under the shadow of it.*

- *Acts 4:13-14 (NIV) When they saw the courage of Peter and John and realized that they were unschooled, ordinary men, they were astonished and they took note that these men had been with JESUS. But since they could see the man who had been healed standing there with them, there was nothing they could say.*

- *Philippians 4:11-15 (KJV) Not that I speak in respect of want: for I have learned, in whatsoever state I am, therewith to be content. I know both how to be abased, and I know how to abound: every where and in all things I am instructed both to be full and to be hungry, both to abound and to suffer need. I can do all things through CHRIST which strengtheneth me.*

Fly With GOD

Can you remember how easy it was to blame your lack of money for not flying? Now it is time for you to answer the question what do you have?

Fuel: Physical Resources for the flight	
What you believe you need to get started?	What you currently have?
1.	1.
2.	2.
3.	3.
4.	4.
5.	5.
6.	6.
7.	7.
8.	8.

Completion Date: ___/ ___/ ____

Chapter 20:
Air Traffic Controller (ATC)

ATC: Provides up-to-the-microsecond flight data which allows instantaneous adjustment for the journey.

In the natural, an Air Traffic Controller (ATC) operates the air traffic control system to expedite and maintain a safe and orderly flow of air traffic while helping to prevent mid-air collisions. ATC has the ability to obtain and relay vital weather information to pilots. Additionally, tries to prevent pilots from coming too close to other pilots and/or objects in the air and on the ground. In the spiritual realm, the HOLY SPIRIT is responsible for all ATC services. HE directs your activities on the ground and in the air which includes spiritual thunderstorms, object avoidance and other Flight Plan changes.

One major difference between the ATCs in the natural verses the spiritual is that the natural ones are always looking for ideal weather conditions to take-off and Fly. ATCs would never send us flying in any type of adverse conditions. If ATCs were looking at our lives, they most likely would have grounded us forever, since our weather conditions, would seldom be ideal for flight. But, our

Fly With GOD

spiritual ATC (HOLY SPIRIT) sees these storms as ideal conditions for perfecting our faith[255] in flight.

You're In The Plane, Ready To Go!

Best Conditions. No matter the weather it is time for you to Fly. GOD has declared it to be the *"Best Conditions"* ever. By best I mean the most advantageous for your spiritual development. GOD wants you to be prepared so it is still important to know as much as you can about your weather forecast prior to your flight. Having as much insight into what is coming your way allow you to take the wisest flight path.

The dictionary defines weather as *"the state of the atmosphere at a given time and place, with respect to variables such as temperature, moisture, wind velocity, and barometric pressure.*[256]*"* So what spiritual atmosphere do you find yourself in today? Has your prayer time revealed sunny skies or tornado warnings? Are the weathermen (prophets) reporting (prophesying) turbulence, storms, rain, high winds, sleet and more? Are they true or false reports?

In the Book of Job, GOD reminds us that HE controls it all; We find Job experiencing what GOD has allowed or could we say Acts of GOD.[257] Whether the skies are calm or treacherous you are in a wonderful place; the center of GOD's will. You are experiencing what the world has called for 100s of years an "Act of GOD." What better place to be, but in the center of GOD's grand performance on earth, no one else is able to steal the show; it is GOD and GOD alone.

As I studied more about an "Act of GOD," I discovered the description was one sided. It seemed that the only "Acts of GOD" the intellects were writing about were the violent or destructive

---

[255] 1 Peter 1:7; 1 Peter 4:12

[256] The American Heritage Dictionary of the English Language, 4th edition, published by Houghton Mifflin Company

[257] Job 37-38

Chapter 20: Air Traffic Controller (atc)

natural forces, that were beyond human power to cause, prevent, or control; such as hurricanes or earthquakes. But what about the sunshine? Isn't that beyond our control, therefore an Act of GOD?

I remember Joshua causing the sun to stand still while the Israelites won the war against the Amorites[258]. The sunshine was truly an Act of GOD. I also recall how Silas and Paul's praying and praising caused an earthquake to open the prison doors and loose their chains[259]. Their freedom was another Act of GOD. Whether we view the conditions positive or negative, they are all "Acts of GOD" and therefore are GOD's best conditions for our journey.

What you learned in the waiting room has produced dividends maturing your faith in action so much, that you will be able to navigate in either calm or treacherous skies. You need only to remember that the prophet Elijah had so much favor with GOD that he was able to tell Ahab when the rain would stop and start; and embarrass Baal's prophets with enough fire to burn a water drenched alter.[260]

So will your faith in action be able to accurately forecast the storms life throws your way? It all depends on your view of the weather. Many Christians have a ground perspective instead of an aerial view. When on the ground the circumstances you are in seem very important and all consuming, but changing your perspective to the sky can make all the difference in whether you Fly or stay on the tarmac.

Your ability to forecast the weather begins with your level of spiritual eyesight. There are two kinds of situations that can limit your aerial view, either Myopia (nearsightedness) and/or Strabismus (crossed eyes). Myopia will stop you from seeing what's in the distance and Strabismus will cause you to focus on the wrong things.

---

[258] Joshua 10:12-14

[259] Acts 16:25-26

[260] 1 Kings 17-18

Fly With GOD

Myopia Perspective. The dictionary defines Myopia as: *"a visual defect in which distant objects appear blurred because their images are focused in front of the retina rather than on it, or nearsightedness, is also called short sightedness, and lack of discernment or long-range perspective in thinking or planning."* [261] A Myopic view will force you to see only what is closest to you. Your decisions will be based on this limited information. If you accomplish lift-off, your focus will still be on your past and/or present. You will always be hovering close to the ground unable to rise into your future.

GOD desires to correct your spiritual vision from myopic to that of an eagle (20/5). 20/5 vision is the best recorded vision possible for humans, it means that we can see things that are 20 feet away as if they are only 5 feet away. This type of vision is considered highly uncommon. GOD wants you to have extraordinary vision. Changing your eyesight begins with opening your eyes and seeing things the way GOD sees them. Often we are so consumed with the forces against us; we cannot see who is for us.[262] GOD's prescription for this condition is fasting, praising and praying your way through it.

Nehemiah, Esther, Jeremiah, Daniel, Joel, Cornelius and the disciples all knew the power of a HOLY SPIRIT filled fast. How sacrifice not only gave them answers, but saved lives. The Old and New Testaments are full of story-after-story of how so many saints were able to hear from GOD. They were able in a matter of days to go from a myopic to having eagle eyes, not only seeing but soaring.

When I was a child I learned an important song that constantly allows me to correct this type of vision. That praise song was *"Count Your Blessings[263]"*:

---

[261] The American Heritage Dictionary of the English Language, 4th edition, published by Houghton Mifflin Company

[262] 1 John 4:4

[263] 1856-1926 John Oatman, 1851-1921 Edwin O.Excell, Words and Music by John Oatman Jr & Edwin O.Excell

Chapter 20: Air Traffic Controller (atc)

> *"Count your blessings, name them one by one, Count your blessings, see what GOD hath done! Count your blessings, name them one by one, and it will surprise you what the LORD hath done."*

Godly gratitude is one of the best ways to correct myopic vision. That song still gives me strength and allows me to see pass my initial circumstances to the bigger picture of my future and to Fly each day.

Praying is another way to correct Myopia. Its power to provide a 20/5 view is best seen in 2 Kings.[264] Here you find a great story about how a servant was able to see his circumstances the way GOD does. When his enemies (the Syrians) had surrounded him, Elisha declared to his fearful servant, "Don't be afraid, those who are with us are more than those who are with them." And Elisha prayed, "O LORD, open his eyes so he may see." Then, the LORD opened the servant's eyes, and he looked and saw the hills full of horses and chariots of fire all around them. Elisha prayed again this time he requested that GOD would blind the Syrians which GOD did and Elisha marched them into Samaria, their enemy's camp. Once in the camp, Elisha prayed again this time for the Syrians eyes to be opened. When they opened their eyes, they were surrounded by their enemy, the King of Israel's army.

Angels always see the victory – They are airborne!

This story holds two important messages for believers about their perspective.

The first is getting the whole truth: If you don't have GOD's view – you're missing the truth about what is actually taking place in both the spiritual and physical realm. The fact the spiritual will always trump the physical. A ground perspective can give you a few facts, but not the ability to see how these small facts play into

---

[264] 2 Kings 6:8-33

Fly With GOD

the landscape that GOD has prepared for you, which is the truth that HIS obedient children always win.

The second point is changing the perspective: A ground perspective can change when a HOLY SPIRIT-filled person prays for a heavenly perspective to take place. Elisha reveals the power of prayer to not only open peoples' eyes, but to close them as well.

Myopia when used properly can benefit your journey. Being a light in the world allows you to be an agent for change in the world. This anointing allows other people's perspective to be changed because of the light you share with them. Elisha is an example of the power of intercessory prayer in moving individuals from a ground perspective to an aerial view; and then an aerial view to a ground perspective in order to Fly.

> The truth is more important than the facts.
>
> Frank Lloyd Wright

Strabismus Perspective. The dictionary defines Strabismus as: *"a visual defect in which the eyes look in different directions and do not focus simultaneously on a single point, also called crossed eyes. It is caused by a lack of coordination between the eyes."*[265] A Strabismus view forces you to look in several directions; ultimately focusing on the wrong matters. Many of us will spend a lifetime on the tarmac instead of actually flying because we are unable to focus our energy on what GOD has called us to do, Fly.

> *On August 7th, 1954 during the British Empire and Commonwealth Games in Vancouver, B.C., Roger Bannister and John Landy met for the first time for the 1 mile run. Both men had beaten the 4 minute mark previously. It would later be known as the "miracle mile." With only 90 yards to go, John*

---

[265]*The American Heritage Dictionary of the English Language,* 4th edition, published by Houghton Mifflin Company

Chapter 20: Air Traffic Controller (atc)

> *Landy glanced over his left shoulder. At that instant, Bannister streaked by on Landy's right to win in a time of 3:58:8. Landy's second place finish of 3:59.6 marked the first time the 4 minute mile had been broken by two runners in the same race.*[266]

Strabismus view caused Landy to focus in the wrong direction and he lost by fractions of a second. I wonder what would have happen if Landy had not looked back; I believe he would have won. Your improper vision can cause you to focus on the wrong thing, just before you win the prize. Often our distractions don't seem as obvious as Mr. Landy's, but nonetheless the results are the same.

A Strabismus distraction forces you to focus on busy work; worry or so many other things. These distractions keep you away from your highest calling. Distractions that continue to stop you from going back to school, getting a new job and/or even helping that neighbor in need. It is eyesight like this which allows you to remain distracted on the tarmac. These distractions can delay your flight for years – if not a lifetime. This dangerous condition permanently or temporarily distracts you from the real mission at hand, which is to Fly.

I gave you Mr. Landy's story, but what about mine. Does any of this sound familiar to you?

> *I have experienced this same syndrome way too often. I know I have an excellent idea—but I need time to work on it. I start each day planning on working on it. I'm all excited the night before, but somehow I get distracted and don't do what I know I should do. So the next day, I come in determined not to be defeated like I was the previous day. I come in to work. I set my day to do the most important things first. But somehow I find a million reasons*

---

[266] http://www.runningplanet.com/catalog/bannister-landy-miracle-mile.html

Fly With GOD

> *not to work on those tasks, so another day passes; living cross-eyed.*

Strabismus' perspective is in fact one of the most deadly challenges to your call to Fly. Every day, millions of godly people are being distracted from doing the mission GOD called them to do. Christians have become experts at multi-tasking; but failures at completing the tasks GOD has personally called them to do. We have become so out of touch with GOD's best that we truly believe "good" is best. This perspective not only distorts your vision, but allows you to believe your eyesight is perfect; so much so, you may ask GOD to support what you see.

All you need to do, to verify this is to look at Mary and Martha in the Book of Luke. Martha thought she was completely right in what she saw. You know this is true —because why else would she have engaged JESUS' assistance to get Mary to help her. Here we have JESUS at Martha and Mary's house for dinner. Martha is so busy cooking and cleaning (being distracted) that she misses the "20/5" view of this moment: JESUS the "King of Kings" is here!

Martha is suffering badly from Strabismus view. She is unable to recognize her own problem. Martha asked JESUS to make her sister Mary help her with her distractions, *"And JESUS answered and said unto her, Martha, Martha, thou art careful and troubled about many things: But one thing is needful: and Mary hath chosen that good part, which shall not be taken away from her."*[267] Here JESUS not only identifies the distraction in Martha's life but clearly displays HIS support for Mary's view.

So how can you Fly in your call instead of being caught up in the numerous distractions that everyday life throws at you? Taking a look at your motives is the best place to start. You need to discover whether you are being motivated to do something good or GOD's best.

---

[267] Luke 10:41-42

Chapter 20: Air Traffic Controller (atc)

Your good job can often distract you from GOD's best job. I believe there are some differentiators that can be used to determine if the task is moving you toward your call instead of a distraction. There are some internal assessment processes that you can utilize to determine if you are operating with the best eyesight. To eliminate stigmas and distractions you will need to conduct your own internal due diligence process to determine if the task is part of a call or just a distraction.

You are capable of doing your own spiritual due diligence. This ability was given to you the moment you were saved. You were given the HOLY SPIRIT at that moment to lead, guide and teach you kingdom living on earth.[268] This wisdom was placed in you when you became born again. You have the ability to expose the root cause of your actions.

Daniel had holy vision. He was most noted for his righteousness and his ability to decipher complicated visions. He sought GOD always for revelation and knowledge. He realized that seeing only presented facts and facts were not enough. He knew only GOD could put those facts into a perspective that allowed truth to be disclosed. Solomon understood it also when he said *"Where there is no vision, the people perish: ..."*[269] He understood vision leads to a mission, a mission leads to goals and they all lead to GOD's BEST.

On the other hand, when you purposely miss the mark out of defiance, then the consequence to your actions may be rejection. The Bible is full of stories that use an anointed individual to disclose the rejected person's ungodly motives. For instance, Samuel is used to reveal Saul's motives. Saul cared more about pleasing man then GOD. He was rejected as king of Israel [270]. Another example is when JESUS is used to reveal the rich man's motives. This man cared

---

[268] John 14:26

[269] Proverbs 29:18

[270] 1 Samuel 15

Fly With GOD

more about wealth then GOD. He missed Heaven[271]. Finally, there is Peter, he is used to reveal Ananias and Sapphira's motives. They cared more about their social standing then GOD. Both fell dead[272].

Only when you get rid of your distractions and turn back to GOD can you move into your calling. HE is waiting for you to repent, so HE can show HIS limitless mercy and move us on our way. King David experienced HIS mercy when he repented from numbering the men. The prophet Gad came to him and told him to raise an altar in the threshingfloor of Araunah the Jebusite.[273] David immediately obeyed and GOD stopped the plague.

To have wings and choose to live on ground level is not GOD's plan for you. HE wants real vision for you. An unbroken view of your entire surrounding, both in the natural and supernatural. In Colossians we are told, *"if we are risen with CHRIST, seek those things which are above, where CHRIST sitteth ... Set your affection on things above, not on things on the earth."*[274]

If the verse above is not a command to have a holy perspective; what is? Here the Apostle Paul reminds you of Christ's resurrection and your inheritance. How you must keep your focus above, not-on-earth, soaring with our LORD and SAVIOR-JESUS CHRIST.

So how is your weather? Are there areas in your life where Myopia has caused you to only see the problems? Or are you suffering from Strabismus, spending a lot of time on things that are not relevant to your flight?

Finally, I have great news for you today, your blessings are closer than they appear. If you miss the mark but are trying diligently, JESUS is standing there in the gap. HE is your bridge from distraction

---

[271] Matthew 19:16-28

[272] Acts 5:1-10

[273] 2 Samuel 24

[274] Colossians 3:1-3

Chapter 20: Air Traffic Controller (atc)

to attraction to GOD. HE sees your heart and your attempts to live a righteous life. The Apostle Paul tells us "because of our fellowship with GOD we need to be confident that the good journey HE started, when you first began packing all the way through lift-off to your destination – HE will complete."[275] GOD provides you with mercy and grace for your distractions. HE will reveal a way out in order for you to Fly.

Dear LORD,

Thank you for allowing me to have YOUR vision. My natural and spiritual eyesight is getting stronger each and every day.

I only believe YOUR report, no matter how long it takes my natural eyes to focus on the truth

In JESUS' name, I pray.

Meditation Scriptures

- *Numbers 13:30 (KJV) And Caleb stilled the people before Moses, and said, Let us go up at once, and possess it; for we are well able to overcome it.*

- *1 Kings 18:41-45 (NIV) And Elijah said to Ahab, "Go, eat and drink, for there is the sound of a heavy rain." So Ahab went off to eat and drink, but Elijah climbed to the top of Carmel, bent down to the ground and put his face between his knees. "Go and look toward the sea," he told his servant. And he went up and looked. "There is nothing there," he said. Seven times Elijah said, "Go back." The seventh time the servant reported, "A cloud as small as a man's hand is rising from the sea." ...sky grew black with clouds, the wind rose, a heavy rain came on and Ahab rode off to Jezreel.*

---

[275] 1 Philippians 1:5-6 (Lily emphasis)

Fly With GOD

Focus on the areas in your life which are spiritually healthy they are your holy view. Explore how you have been able to cultivate those areas. Now think about your unhealthy areas and place them either in the Myopic or Strabismus column.

Your Weather Forecast		
Holy View	Myopic View	Strabismus View
1.	1.	1.
2.	2.	2.
3.	3.	3.
4.	4.	4.
5.	5.	5.
6.	6.	6.
7.	7.	7.
8.	8.	8.

Completion Date: ___/___/____

Part 7: Airborne

If you don't get in that plane you'll regret it. Maybe not today, maybe not tomorrow, but soon and for the rest of your life.

— Rick Blaine in the movie Casablanca.

YOU'RE FLYING

Not by might, nor by power, but by MY spirit, saith the LORD of hosts.

Zechariah 4:6

Chapter 21: Understanding Aerodynamics

AERODYNAMICS —It is a unique combination of forces that GOD provides or allows which moves you through the air.

Taxi Down the Runway. Taxiing down the runway is meant to be an exhilarating experience full of GOD's favor. You have gotten the call, packed, studied and now it is time. You are finally ready. All those days, weeks, or years you spent waiting in the terminal preparing and becoming teachable has left you able to override that self-doubt conversation with powerful working faith. So you start praising GOD even more and try not to dance out of your clothes. It is time to sit down and buckle-up.

Fasten Your Seatbelt!

Once seated, you securely place the spiritual seatbelt around your waist pulling it as tight as you can. The seatbelt will keep you safe and secure in case of sudden altitude change – the Bible calls them trials.[276] The seatbelt represents the ability to *"stand firm ... with the belt of truth buckled around your waist.[277]"*

---

[276] 1 Peter 4:12-13

[277] Ephesians 6:14 NIV

Fly With GOD

Everything you have been able to surrender to GOD has led you to such a time as this.[278] All you have studied, applied, and completed has brought you to this very moment of spiritual safety and security. The question now is, not whether you are meant to Fly, but—when, where and how high. Inside you are the secrets to your innate ability to Fly, not just once, but to sustain your flight, moving from one destination to the next.

Before your plane came off the assembly line, GOD declared you as ready to Fly – wonderfully made. HE said, HIS works are marvelous![279] All – you're required to do is have faith in GOD and begin. You are not a lemon. You have been checked and inspected by GOD himself. HE not only spoke it into existence, but made sure you were ready to Fly.

You and I face Flying-decisions thousands of times a day. The decision to Fly or continue to Fly is made every moment. Your freewill allows you to turn toward or away from GOD at a moment's notice, to either continue your flight or abort it. The choice is always yours.

Peter is a great example of how things can change in a moment when you start focusing on the weather (your conditions). One minute, Peter has his eyes on JESUS and he is walking on water; and the next moment his eyes are on the weather, instead of JESUS and he begins to sink.[280] It only took a second for Peter to start descending into the sea, once he took his eyes off of JESUS. But the good news for you, just like for Peter, the instant you change your focus to GOD; you begin flying again. So here are my questions:

> Is your seatbelt fastened?
> Is your flight plan approved?
> *Is there gas in your tank?*

---

[278]Esther 4:14

[279]Psalm 139:14

[280]Matthew 14:28-31

Chapter 21: Understanding Aerodynamics

If all your answers are YES – It is time for you to start *"Taxiing Down the Runway."* Everything has been checked and rechecked; all systems are go! You have followed the right path and listened to all the travelling instructions given in Ephesians.[281] You have: truth, righteousness, peace, faith, salvation and the Word of GOD for your mission.

The fact that planes are leaving all the time doesn't matter. It is up to you to Fly your own race. The only thing that matters right now is that the ATC has just called your flight number.

> *You are now speeding down the runway. All lights are green. You start feeling the wind beneath your wings and the plane vibrating. You're so excited; you know that you are almost off the ground. Just one more push; you'll have lift-off. WOW what a wonderful feeling!*

Steady-State. WOW – what a feeling, you are now finally in the air. At this moment you are in total ecstasy. You promise yourself that you will always do whatever it takes to stay in this moment, no matter what it cost. In aerodynamic terms you have reached your *"Steady-State"* of flight. This is when the altitude, direction, and speed remain constant until a force or forces change in magnitude. Simply said, you are cruising through the air with ease.

This period of cruising is often brief, not lasting long, since the various forces affecting you are seldom static. Some of the negative elements that impacted you before take-off may return and/or new ones will arise. Areas that seemed wonderful when you began your journey will now require you to balance them with competing priorities.

How will you adjust for changing forces, flying high while staying in that wonderful *"Steady-State?"* I'm sorry to say: "YOU CAN'T"!

---

[281]Ephesians 6:13-19

Fly With GOD

Flying high requires some level of turbulence. The type of turbulence the Bible calls a test, a trial, or even tribulation.[282]

By understanding the aerodynamic forces required to initiate, sustain, and soar you will at best be able to minimize your level of turbulence. These forces in the natural are called Lift, Weight, Thrust and Drag. The *"Lift"* pulls the plane upward; the *"Weight"* pulls the plane downward; the *"Thrust"* pulls the plane forward; and finally the *"Drag"* pulls the plane backward.

These four forces are necessary for a plane to remain airborne. These forces act as counterbalances; a weight balancing another weight. This counterbalance allows the plane to either soar or stall depending on the amount of pressure exerted by each force.

Natural	Spiritual
Lift	GOD
Weight	Relationship
Thrust	Ministry
Drag	Till

There are four forces in Christian flight: GOD, Relationship, Ministry and Till. These spiritual forces align directly to the natural forces exerting their form of pressure on the flight.

The GOD—force is always present, before the world existed and after. The first line in the Bible says, *"In the beginning God created the heaven and the earth."*[283] And the GOD—force is never-ending as detailed in Revelation 1:4 *"... from HIM which is, and which was, and which is to come"*.

The Relationship—force first appeared on the 6th day of creation when GOD created Adam then Eve; *"So GOD created man in his*

---

[282] 1 Peter 4:12, Romans 5:3

[283] Genesis 1:1

own image, in the image of GOD created HE him; male and female created HE them."[284]

The Ministry—force took on a new dimension after the resurrection of JESUS CHRIST when JESUS told the 11 disciples to *"Go ye therefore, and teach all nations, baptizing them in the name of the Father, and of the Son, and of the Holy Ghost: Teaching them to observe all things whatsoever I have commanded you: and, lo, I am with you always, even unto the end of the world."*[285] At this point, every born-again Christian is called into ministry.

The Till—force started when Adam and Eve were sent out of the Garden of Eden for their sin. GOD said, *"Therefore the LORD God sent him forth from the garden of Eden, to till the ground from whence he was taken."*[286]

These forces are interdependent. Their influence acts in opposition, constantly affecting your flying altitude and speed. The *"GOD—force"* pulls you upward; the *"Relationship—force"* pulls you downward; the *"Ministry—force"* pulls you forward; and finally, the *"Till—force"* pulls you backward. The *"GOD—force"* is the only force that will always bring you up. It is capable of acting as an enzyme changing the direction of the other three forces. It is the only force of the 4-forces that is omnipresent.

Each force is important for flight. These forces are seldom equally distributed causing the altitude, speed and directions to change based on their pull. Most of the time, you find yourself favoring one force or over another; and/or compensating to correct the effects of a particular force. Your optimum performance in the air is based completely on your force stewardship; the ability to manage your life while responding to the various forces affecting flight.

---

[284]Genesis 1:27

[285]Matthew 28:16-20

[286]Genesis 3:23

Fly With GOD

As Christians, you often desire that the Lift (GOD—Force) and the Thrust (Ministry—Force) would flow in such a manner to smoothly increase speed while increasing altitude. But, life seldom works like that. You may find yourself spending too much time with your friends which increases your Relationship—Force directly affecting your GOD, Ministry, and/or Till—forces. Thus, your stewardship skills will determine your ability to reach and sustain optimum performance while enjoying the journey.

Flying too slow may mean you have put too much emphasis on Till, which is now dragging you quickly backward at the expense of the other forces. In the natural, this exertion would cause the plane to literally start falling from the sky. As a Christian the effects are similar: fatigue, exhaustion, depression, illness, and/or premature death.

It is your duty, as a skillful pilot, to manage your flight between each one of these forces. But first you must understand the composition of each force and then the complexities of the aerodynamic properties that allow them to operate; simply put—how these forces interact. All of these forces will assist you in arriving at your destination. You are continuously wrestling with these 4-forces while you are airborne. Jacob in Genesis 12[287] is a reminder of how we wrestle to see GOD and be blessed.

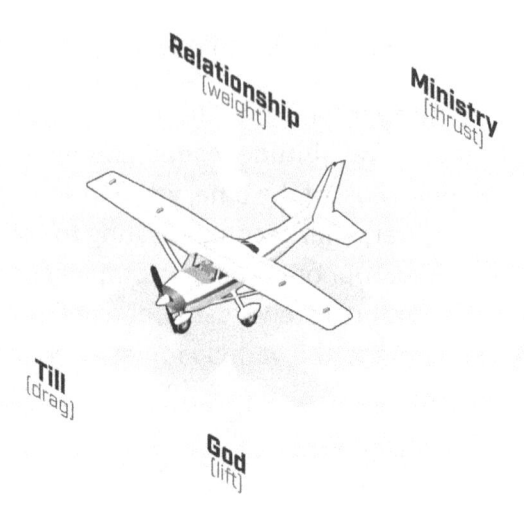

Relationship [weight]

Ministry [thrust]

Till [drag]

God [lift]

---

[287] Genesis 32:22-29

What is the GOD—force? The GOD—force is analogous to the lift force that affects the top of an aircraft. This force was the hardest for me to define, I was truly wrestling with how to describe it. It took me a long time to figure out how and what I was to say about the GOD—force. When I finally stopped resting on my own understanding, GOD reminded me of HIS response to Moses, *"I AM THAT I AM."*[288] Even then GOD was telling HIS people that HE would not be put in a box.

This is where you get glimpses of how awesome and wonderful GOD is. The journey of understanding how much GOD is truly out-of-the-box. I believe it took me so long to finish this book because every time I reread a chapter, I had to make the box bigger [therefore more editing] based on GOD evolving me. I needed to only do a roll call of some of GOD's commonly used names and attributes throughout the Bible to confirm my evolution:

FATHER

The First and Last

Alpha & Omega

Elohim (Covenant & Creative)

El Shaddai (All Sufficient)

Adonai (Master)

Jehovah Jireh (Provider)

Jehovah Rophe (Healer)

Jehovah Nissi (Banner)

Jehovah M'Kaddesh (Santifies)

Jehovah Shalom (Peace)

Jehovah Tsidkenu (Righteousness)

Jehovah Shammah (Here)

---

[288]Exodus 3:13-14

Fly With GOD

The GOD—force shows HIS Glory.[289] In chapter 30 of Exodus, you will find Moses once again asking GOD a critical question, *"to show him HIS Glory."* GOD denies him his request. For Moses to see GOD's face in his mortal state would require his flesh to die, which means he would be dead. Simply said, his mission on earth would be finished—on to HEAVEN!

In order for you to operate in your earthly state for the kingdom, you retain some of your fleshy nature. There is in effect a type of struggle between GOD and your other forces (Relationship, Work, and Ministry). This struggle as mentioned earlier is called a counterbalance[290] and it determines just how much of GOD's glory will be revealed during your journey.

Jacob was a great example of the power of the GOD—force. He was born holding his brother Esau's foot. Jacob stole both Esau's birthright and blessing. When Esau swears to kill Jacob for his actions, Jacob swiftly leaves home. While Jacob is separated from his immediate family – he matures, the GOD—force becomes stronger and stronger. Finally, Jacob at the brook of Peniel understands how crucial the GOD—force is to Aerodynamics. He wrestles all night to insure he stays airborne.[291]

On the other-hand, Enoch's story reveals a man whose GOD—force was completely revealed. We don't read about him ever wrestling with GOD. Enoch never saw death. Enoch pleased GOD so much; GOD took him to be with HIM without Enoch having to experience death in order to obtain eternal life with HIM.[292]

Moses, Jacob and Enoch's journeys reveal how the GOD—force is tempered showing you portions of HIS glory based on how much

---

[289] Exodus 33

[290] Counterbalance in this text is defined as the weight of another force or forces which in general are of equal weight, force, or influence.

[291] Genesis 25, 27, and 32:23-34

[292] Genesis 5:24, Hebrews 11:5

Chapter 21: Understanding Aerodynamics

of your worldly self is dead. As confirmed by the Apostle Paul, GOD in CHRIST with ALL HIS Glory and Righteousness is reserved for your immortal state; no flesh will glory in HIS presence.[293] The Bible is full of individuals that had to wrestle with the GOD-force to sustain flight. Below are a few individuals from the Bible who won or lost when their response to the GOD-force was tested.

GOD—force

Positive Examples	Citation
Abraham willingness to sacrifice Isaac.	Genesis 22:5-10
Gideon taking only the men which lapped the water to battle.	Judges 7
JESUS doing only what the FATHER commanded.	New Testament
Negative Examples	**Citation**
Prophet listened to a senior prophet instead of GOD.	1 Kings 13:7-24
Jonah not going to Nineveh.	Jonah 1
Martha preparing food instead of fellowship with JESUS.	Luke 10:38-42

As mentioned earlier, a mortal state could only partake of a portion of the GOD—force. This portion changed with the sacrifice of JESUS CHRIST. When the temple's veil was torn humankind was given the opportunity to have complete access to GOD through HIS son JESUS CHRIST.

---

[293] 1 Corinthians 1:29; That no flesh should glory in his presence.

Fly With GOD

What is the Relationship —force? The Relationship—force is analogous to the weight force that affects the bottom of a plane. Your relationship with people, places or things have an effect on your ability to Fly. Environmental factors such as home, neighborhood, crime, education, cost of living, pollution, commerce, technology and much more. All these factors contribute to the Relationship—force. There are thousands of daily external and internal factors that affect your ability to Fly high or low. They began the moment you were conceived and will continue until you die.

The Relationship—force equals the sum total of the impact of your contacts, associations, and involvements. This includes people, places and things. If you have a mobile device or television, you are bombarded with information telling you that you need more things; more money to buy them, more space to house them and more time to use them.

You are constantly being told that there is something wrong with you if you don't know more people or acquire more things. Thus, if you satisfy even one of those needs you might become one of the millions of Christians that have, or will have a toxic relationship with social media, alcohol, cigarettes, drugs, food, shopping or any of the other addictive behaviors known to humankind. The impact of the Relationship—force plays a major role in how your altitude will adjust on a second-by-second basis.

For many, our first flight adjustment came from our family. Maybe a brother or sister told us that we were not smart enough to become a doctor or lawyer. Maybe they said just the opposite, that we were brilliant and could do anything we wanted to do. Our family's interaction with us may have affected how we acted in the past and possibly how we act today. Family, friends, acquaintances and even enemies contribute to our Relationship—force. They all can have an impact on whether we soar or fall.

The Bible is full of individuals that were impacted by the Relationship—force. Like I said earlier in the chapter, the

Chapter 21: Understanding Aerodynamics

"GOD—force" is capable of acting as an enzyme changing the direction of the Relationship—force from going down to up. This happens when GOD steps in. Below are a few individuals from the Bible which found their response to the Relationship—force tested.

Relationship—force

Positive Examples	Citation
Moses hands were kept up by Aaron and Hur to bring Israelites victory over the Amalekites.	Exodus 17:12
Esther being mentored by Mordecai.	Book of Esther
Paralytic man's friends lowering him through the roof.	Mark 2:3-5
Negative Examples	**Citation**
Eve listening to the serpent.	Genesis 3
Samson falling in love with and trusting Delilah.	Judges 16
David committing adultery with Bathsheba.	2 Samuel 11-12

Relationships are important to your ability to flourish. Your challenge is to develop and invest in only the relationships GOD has created to glorify HIM. In Genesis, GOD was so concerned about Adam being lonely HE created living creatures and Eve to satisfy Adam's relationship need. These were relationships which GOD had picked for Adam. I believe GOD has hand-picked relationships for you.

What is the Ministry —force? This Ministry—force is analogous to the thrust force that affects the forward motion of an aircraft. In the spiritual realm it is the things you gain for the kingdom. This book defines it as the "Good News or New Testament" in action.

Fly With GOD

JESUS said it best, *"everything we do for the least of them, you did for HIM."*[294]

We <u>will not</u> focus on the traditional definition of ministry (religious activities, clergy, religious vocation, etc.). The *"Old Testament"* laws, offerings, animal sacrifices, vows, etc.; humankind's way of having fellowship with the LORD.

The "New Testament" reveals a powerful Ministry—force. Once, JESUS CHRIST died and was resurrected the Ministry—force changed from a book of laws to one of love. The unbelievable love JESUS CHRIST has for you. The New Testament reveals a covenant stressing a life of loving and giving. The Ministry—force was part of GOD's plan to cancel Adam and Eve's sin in the Garden of Eden bringing humankind back to full fellowship with the LORD.

This book will define ministry much broader than many dictionaries. Ministry will be defined as the ability to possess, settle, or use land or property at our current station for GOD's service.[295] The traditional definition is such a small part of what I consider the Ministry—force to be composed of. The definition I have provided directly lines up with the Apostle Paul's statement in the Book of Corinthians to become a living epistle for the LORD. Therefore, Ministry—force is the integration through action of CHRIST in both our relationships and deeds.[296]

How you live daily is our ministry—not how we live on the Sabbath day! Our actions at work, home and in the neighborhood is our ministry. Every waking moment we are in ministry. It is what we give back to others; good or bad. We are to let our light shine so our works will glorify the LORD.[297]

---

[294]Matthew 25:39-41

[295]Ephesians 4:12

[296]2 Corinthians 3:2-4

[297]Matthew 5:16

Ministry—force is not the 3.6%[298] of our time spent on Sabbath day. It is not that loving person we become when working in our church. It is the life that we publish to the world during our every waking moment. This force is focused on the godly work we accomplish to bring people into the saving knowledge of JESUS CHRIST. With so much work to do for the kingdom, it is clear to me, that GOD would have never left such an important mission for just the Sabbath day. That's why I believe as JESUS' final assignment, before HE ascended to Heaven was the Great Commission. HE told us to go into "... all the world, and preach the gospel to every creature."[299] If JESUS were here today, I believe we would have called this a "Drop the Mic" moment! HE is calling us all out to meet HIM!

Ministry—force much like everything else must be built on the right motives to work. Matthew reminds you that in the end the LORD will review your actions to make sure of your motives. Were you doing it to look important or was it truly about GOD's will?[300]

Whatever you do to increase territory at work or in your relationships is a part of the Ministry—force. In Corinthians, you are given the example of how planting and watering play an integral part in ministry, but only GOD can give the increase.[301] Isn't it great to know that you need not be concerned about how big a part you play as long as you remain a living epistle of the LORD's sovereignty and FLY.

The Bible is full of individuals that were impacted by the Ministry—force to sustain flight. Below are a few individuals from the Bible and their response to the Ministry—force.

---

[298]This assumes eight (8) hours of sleep and Sabbath services which last for four (4) hours

[299]Mark 16:14-20

[300]Matthew 7:22

[301]1 Corinthians 3

Fly With GOD

Ministry—force

Positive Examples	Citation
JESUS's birth, sacrifice, and resurrection.	New Testament
Stephen's preaching, arrest, and stoning.	Act 6-7
Dorcas always doing good work and helping the poor.	Acts 9:36

Negative Examples	Citation
Church in Laodicea was lukewarm to GOD.	Revelation 3:14-22
Saul persecuting the Christians.	Acts 9
Jonah fleeing to Tarshish.	Book of Jonah

What is the Till —force? The Till—force is analogous to the drag force that affects the back of an aircraft. It reduces the lift on the plane. In the spiritual realm it is the consequence that occurred when Adam and Eve were ejected from Eden. Humankind had to transition from a work which was full of creativity, fun and joy, to one of tilling, sorrow and often suffering[302] which I call the Till—force.

In Genesis, GOD gave humankind their initial work assignment, *"And God blessed them, and God said unto them, be fruitful, and multiply, and replenish the earth, and subdue it: and have dominion over the fish of the sea, and over the fowl of the air, and over every living thing that moveth upon the earth.[303]"* After a rebellious act, GOD modified[304] the work assignment from being blessed to cursed, "...cursed is the ground for thy sake; in sorrow shalt thou eat of it all the days of thy life"; work went from constant pleasure, to being hard and often painful.

In the beginning work was part of our divine relationship. I believe when GOD created humankind the word for "work" was full of

---

[302]Genesis 3

[303]Genesis 1:28

[304]Genesis 3:17-19

Chapter 21: Understanding Aerodynamics

imagination, creativity and abundant joy. We only need to look at how work was described in the beginning to know this is true. GOD rested from an awe-inspiring work experience. HE had designed a world where we could fellowship with HIM all day long. Upon the ejection of Adam and Eve the definition of work went from "awe-inspiring" to one of "tilling". We had to dig and search for, what was totally available in Eden.

Till being the sweaty activities in which a person is engaged in to produce or accomplish a task. The Till—force is the activity, assignment, attempt, commission, endeavor, performance, production, striving, struggle, and undertaking of physical and/or mental labor needed for us to fill and subdue the earth after the fall.

Adam and Eve's sin changed our job description, but JESUS CHRIST has interceded on our behalf. We were chosen to live off the fat of the land, not the lack of the land. It is important for you as a Christian to understand that GOD personally fashioned each one of us uniquely to complete various tasks on earth. When you are fully engaged in that task, you shift from the Till—force to the other three (3) forces depending on your assignment. The difference can move you from pain to joy, sickness to wholeness, weakness to strength, and/or poverty to abundance.

A great example of the Till-Force is in Luke 5. Simon had been fishing all night; sweating, struggling and striving to catch fish with no results "tilling". JESUS ask Simon for the use of his boat. When Simon says yes, he is immediately shifted into the Ministry-Force. After JESUS uses Simon's boat, he is instructed to go back into the deep. An awe-inspiring GOD journey which results in more fish than he or his friends can imagine.

On the other-hand, the wealthy young man who inquires about obtaining eternal life is a great example of the Till—force. This man spent his entire life working hard to gain wealth and making sure to follow all the commandments. He doesn't realize—he is working under the curse that resulted from Adam and Eve's fall. JESUS confronts the "drag" on his life. HE tells him to sell all, give it

Fly With GOD

to the poor and follow HIM. But the rich young man sadly decides to continue to "Till"[305] instead of Flying.

Often the Till—force is thought of as our principal work or business, our means of earning a livelihood; but it is much greater. It is our particular thoughts and actions regarding occupation, business, profession, and calling; all rolled into one force. It may even include how we dread Mondays, sales reports, appraisals, and people. The Till—force converts to the Ministry—force when you submit your will to GOD as HE requested in Eden. When JESUS ascended to Heaven, HE made provisions for your work on earth. The blessing of Eden, work which is full of imagination, creativity and abundant joy. It is up to you to make sure that your thoughts and actions are what GOD purposed in you. To either follow the positive or negative examples below:

Till—force

Positive Examples	Citation
Noah builds the Ark	Genesis 7-9
Solomon built the temple	1 Kings 5-6
Nehemiah rebuilds the wall	Book Nehemiah

Negative Examples	Citation
Martha prepares dinner instead of sitting with JESUS	Luke 10:40-42
Mankind Builds the Tower of Babel to reach Heaven instead of seeking GOD	Genesis 11
David takes census of fighting men instead of leaning on GOD	1 Chronicles 21

---

[305]Matthew 19:16-22

Chapter 21: Understanding Aerodynamics

Force Summary. The opposite forces interact the most. GOD gave Adam everything including HIMSELF. Adam was given freewill to determine what forces would have the greatest impact on his life. GOD made you in HIS image and believes that you are capable of keeping HIM above all the other forces. It is up to you—to love the GIVER more than the gifts, in order to Fly high.

Dear LORD,

Allow me to stay in the center of YOUR will.

Let me always remember that no matter what force comes my way that all things work together for good because I have been called for YOUR purpose

In JESUS CHRIST – Amen

Meditation Scriptures

- *Romans 8:28 (KJV) And we know that all things work together for good to them that love GOD, to them who are the called according to his purpose.*

- *1 Corinthians 15:57-58 (NIV) But thanks be to GOD! HE gives us the victory through our LORD JESUS CHRIST. Therefore, my dear brothers, stand firm. Let nothing move you. Always give yourselves fully to the work of the LORD, because you know that your labor in the LORD is not in vain.*

Fly With GOD

Under the GOD—force section several names of GOD were listed. Take some time to review those names. Which names do you find yourself thinking about most—and why?

Names of GOD	Impact of the Name

Completion Date: ___/ ___/ ___

Chapter 21: Understanding Aerodynamics

How are you balancing the following forces?

Till—force Tasks	Ministry—force Tasks
1.	1.
2.	2.
3.	3.
4.	4.
5.	5.
6.	6.
7.	7.
8.	8.
9.	9.
10.	10.

Completion Date: ___/___/___

Chapter 22:
Your Engine "The Heart"

ENGINE: Converts spiritual energy into physical manifestations; power to produce Flight.

Each day thousands of planes lift tons of weight off the ground with ease. This is made possible by their jet engines. The engine has the ability to suck air in, compress it, treat it, and finally blast it out; thrusting the aircraft forward and upward. Our spiritual Heart is our engine, it allows us to obtain lift-off and soar within the four—forces of flight. To Fly with GOD our engine or should I say Heart, must be spiritually fit. When our Heart is fit, it will have the capacity to move us forward and upward with unbelievable force. This great power will allow us to Fly fast and high.

GOD mentions the Heart, "our engine," over 800 times in the King James Version of the Bible. The Heart's condition is constantly used as an indication as to whether man is grounded or soaring with the LORD. The Old and New Testaments are filled with stories of people having various Heart abnormalities and having them restored by a word and/or a touch from the LORD. Whether it was King Nebuchadnezzar repenting for boasting about how he built Babylon or the Apostle Peter after denying JESUS three times, both their engines were eventually restored. GOD has a knack for showing up at any time during our journey to eliminate blockage.

Chapter 22: Your Engine "the Heart"

HE especially likes showing up at lift-off to insure our engine is at HIS factory setting.

In order for your engine to run at optimum performance, or should I say at the factory setting, you must allow GOD to dismantle it and put it back together HIS way and in HIS time. That is because our ways have often not been HIS ways. King David understood the challenges which occur when you have a Heart condition. After sinning with Bathsheba, he asked to *"Hide thy face from my sins, and blot out all mine iniquities. Create in me a clean heart, O GOD; and renew a right spirit within me. Cast me not away from thy presence; and take not thy HOLY SPIRIT from me...The sacrifices of GOD are a broken spirit: a broken and a contrite heart."*[306] He knew that in order to Fly with GOD his Heart would have to be cleansed from those sins. GOD would have to restore his Heart back to the factory setting.

During the journey, King David also came to realize that Heart trouble can happen again and again. Remember, the 70,000 men who died because he counted the military forces. King David's Heart was not right with the LORD then either. An overhaul, remanufacturing, and/or brokenness must continually take place on the inside for you to become healed and able to hear and act on GOD's commands to Fly. An engine must be inspected for blockages or the engine will either be sluggish or stall, unable to efficiently respond to GOD's commands.

I like the way Apostle Peter explains how to obtain an internal brokenness in his letter to the various churches in Asia Minor. It is clear we need our hearts flowing with a constant supply of the precious blood of JESUS to Fly. Apostle Peter said:

> *"Be holy, because I am holy. Since you call on a FATHER who judges each man's work impartially, live your lives as strangers here in reverent fear. For*

---

[306] Psalm 51:9-11, 17

Fly With GOD

> *you know that it was not with perishable things such as silver or gold that you were redeemed from the empty way of life handed down to you from your forefathers, but with the precious blood of CHRIST, a lamb without blemish or defect."* [307]

Blockage. We are reminded it is only through the Blood of JESUS can our Hearts "be whole—be holy". So what stops your engine or Heart from working properly? A blockage! The result of a progressive buildup of sludge which can clog, break down and damage your Heart. Sludge is the ungodly deposit in our hearts which separate us from the abundant life JESUS told us about.[308] Sludge is the gruel or paste that has slipped into our spirits which left untreated can block our hearts. If these items are allowed to fester they can harden our spiritual hearts and restrict or maybe even block our flight.

Sludge may have been caused by untreated abuses that started in the womb and continued through adulthood, or even something that happened today. The blockage may even have been self-inflicted by what Galatians 5 refers to as "...kind of life which develops out of trying to get your own way all the time: repetitive, loveless, cheap sex; a stinking accumulation of mental and emotional garbage; frenzied and joyless grabs for happiness ..."[309]

In the spirit, sludge is formed every time you turn away from GOD for an instant. Some are so tiny you will hardly notice them; some are so large you may have to change churches to hide them. As Christians, every day we are bombarded with things that can cause us to build-up deposits in our spiritual hearts. This sludge works as a thief trying to steal, kill and destroy what has been promised by

---

[307] 1 Peter 1:16-19

[308] John 10:10

[309] Galatians 5:18-19 (MSG)

Chapter 22: Your Engine "the Heart"

GOD. Even the best saints have had some deposits in their hearts (engines) at one time or the other.

The Priest Eli and the Prophet Samuel were examples of how a blockage can cause a flight to crash or soar.[310] Eli mentored Samuel the prophet who anointed the first king of Israel.[311] Both Eli and Samuel had wicked men in their lives. For Eli it was his two sons Hophni and Phinehas – for Samuel it was King Saul. Both Eli and Samuel were grieved by these men's wicked behavior but only Samuel got rid of the blockage and honored GOD.

King David was called a man after GOD's own heart[312] and he suffered from sludge too. The blockage that he is most noted for is when he committed adultery with Bathsheba and killed her husband to conceal the pregnancy from their affair. Then there was his prideful act – taking a census of the fighting men[313]. The adultery/murder led to the death of his son and the census led to the death of 70,000 people. This blockage derailed his flight, but because the deposits were eventually treated, King David was not permanently grounded.

The prophet Jeremiah was so moved with the amount of sludge mankind can build up, he declared, "The heart is deceitful above all things, and desperately wicked: who can know it?"[314] Only GOD can! GOD's response to Jeremiah is that HE alone has a treatment plan for mankind's Heart – HIM.

---

[310] 1 Samuel 2-3

[311] 1 Samuel 10

[312] 1 Samuel 13:14

[313] 2 Samuel 24:1-9

[314] Jeremiah 17:9

Who Can Know the Heart of Man?

GOD says, "I can and I will reward based on what I see."[315] It doesn't matter to GOD if our blockage is a result of being a victim or victimizer. GOD knows our Heart. HE made a way to eliminate any blockage with the death and resurrection of JESUS CHRIST. HE allowed HIS body to be broken (bruised and beaten) so that our blockages could be broken. HE provides us glimpses of what HE sees every time we come into HIS presence with a broken heart and a contrite spirit.[316] GOD sees our Heart through—The Blood of JESUS.[317]

Treatment. HIS treatment plan pronounces a blessing of brokenness on our ungodly ways. Those ungodly ways which have caused our engine to be sludge ridden are exposed when we fellowship with the LORD. There is an internal brokenness which enables us to function at GOD's best. The brokenness, we experience was designed to cause our Heart valves to either be blocked or leak—leading us back to the MANUFACTURER. Over 2,000 years ago, the Prophet Jeremiah revealed the MANUFACTURER's treatment plan in this scripture:

"For I know the plans I have for you," declares the LORD, "plans to prosper you and not to harm you, plans to give you hope and a future. Then you will call upon me and come and pray to me, and I will listen to you. You will seek me and find me when you seek me with all your heart."[318]

The Prophet reveals what happens to the deposits when you seek the LORD with all your Heart. The plans HE has for you to prosper and not to harm, clearly means that you will Fly high and not crash.

---

[315] Jeremiah 17:10

[316] Psalm 34:18 (lily)

[317] Luke 22:20

[318] Jeremiah 29:11-13 (NIV)

The LORD's supper is a reminder that JESUS made a holy sacrifice for our sins. We no longer have to experience anything that blocks HIS blood from pumping in our hearts. When our Heart is fixed by the LORD, the sludge that was attached to our healthy tissue becomes exposed as evil and malignant. Enabling each one of us to use the spiritual weapons GOD talks about in Ephesians to destroy and crush the enemy that has been responsible for this progressive build-up.[319] These enemies are defeated and the precious blood once again flows freely through our spiritual hearts.

The chief mechanic, "GOD" has treatment plans for you much like HE had for the father with the demon possessed son.[320] This man asked not only for healing for his son but that he would overcome any unbelief. This man not only represents physical brokenness for many Christians, but spiritual brokenness as well. JESUS not only healed his afflicted son but the father now had powerful yoke-breaking belief. He experienced the DELIVERER, the HEALER, the GOD that heals us and makes us whole – JEHOVAH MEPHALTI[321], JEHOVAH ROPHE[322]. What we need, what we desire, what will bless us has always been there; it is JESUS.

When your spiritual Heart is somehow blocked, a spiritual pump may be necessary to unclog it. This spiritual process brings together prayer warriors to breakdown the obstructions. The father with the demon possessed son, first tried to obtain help from the disciples. The disciples tried to heal his son but to no avail. They later question JESUS on why they were unable to cast the spirit out. HE replied that, this kind can come forth by nothing, but by prayer and fasting.[323] By prayer and fasting GOD's power is released – pumping out the sludge and repairing the damage.

---

[319]Ephesians 6:12

[320]Mark 9:17-29

[321]Psalm 18:2

[322]Isaiah 53:4-5

[323]Mark 9:29

Fly With GOD

Earlier Jeremiah tells us to call and pray to GOD, and HE will listen. But he does not quite tell us the form the prosperous answer will take. Thus, I want to be very careful here to underscore the **unclogging** I'm writing about is the "prospering required for your call." Oftentimes the "prospering" GOD gives doesn't line up with what you thought you needed. GOD has promised to fully equip the saints for their jobs, the "prospering" is always the amount needed to Fly. To "equip you with everything good for doing HIS will, and may HE work in us what is pleasing to HIM through JESUS CHRIST to whom be glory …"[324] This is why we see so many different examples of unclogging in the Bible.

I imagine that Paul's "thorn in the flesh" was like his engine running rough in flight. His pump needed to be turned to the "on" position to send a signal to his Heart, correcting its pace. GOD has a way of adjusting our pace, modifying our engines to make sure the pressure is exerted at the right place and time. I believe the answer to why Paul was not healed, lies in whether the blockage actually helped Paul accomplish his call. Paul says further in that chapter that he asked GOD three times to take it away until he realized that it was in fact strengthening him for his journey. This blockage reminded him of the risk of not flying high without continuous treatment. He actually said that he took pleasure in his infirmities. So Paul's answer was YES! He prospered, but in GOD's way, not man's way.

Paul's "healing" is a great example of GOD's master plan; a rough ride which made him strong enough to accomplish his call and to soar! So when you are your weakest, you too can say you are strong; because only then is GOD strongest in your life. HE is also saying to you *"My grace is sufficient for thee: for my strength is made perfect in weakness."*[325]

---

[324] Hebrews 13:21 (NIV)

[325] 2 Corinthians 12:9

Chapter 22: Your Engine "the Heart"

In Paul's case a rough engine was GOD's best. Paul provides us a glimpse of how GOD operates in the spiritual realm; but only a glimpse, because GOD still chooses what and when, HE will reveal. In Paul's case GOD used his brokenness to heal others. GOD may want to use some area in your life to help others. You will only be sure when you seek GOD with all your Heart. If you're seeking, I believe you will experience the strength and peace that the Apostle Paul lived and flew in.

On the other hand, GOD may use broken people to heal you. Some of these same people may never experience healing; that true strength and peace GOD wants to give them. They have been given the message, but never seek it for themselves. The knowledge without application will never lead you to healing. These people have been hardened. They never realize that they are also sick and thus will never experience the treatment that you will receive as you keep your engine charged.

Soaring. You need to be constantly on guard to insure your engine is always in the super-charged mode, able and ready to soar. By pressing into the LORD your engine will remain super-charged. A super-charged engine is always ready for use – it knows the LORD has plans to prosper it and give it hope and a future.[326] You will experience HIS healing power in every aspect of your life: spiritually, physically, and emotionally.

GOD will provide the healing needed to accomplish the call that HE has placed on your life. Galatians will help you understand more about GOD's healing nature in all aspects of your life. It says *"But what happens when we live GOD's way? HE brings gifts into our lives, much the same way that fruit appears in an orchard – things like affection for others, exuberance about life, serenity. We develop a willingness to stick with things, a sense of compassion in the heart, and a conviction that a basic holiness permeates things*

---
[326]Jeremiah 29:11-15 Lily emphasis

Fly With GOD

and people. We find ourselves involved in loyal commitments, not needing to force our way in life, able to marshal and direct our energies wisely. Legalism is helpless in bringing this about; it only gets in the way."[327] This is what it means to have your engine in a constant supercharged mode with a singleness of Heart with your LORD.

As I come to a close, I can only think about the type of soaring that took place throughout history when men and women sought GOD with all their hearts.

- David was called a man after GOD's own heart, not perfect but seeking GOD's will.[328]
- Hezekiah life was extended by GOD because of his heart and prays.[329]
- Ruth was given a husband and child because of her heart for GOD.[330]
- Paul guided people from spiritual and natural drowning because of his heart for GOD.[331]

It is time to daily seek GOD with all your Heart. It is your time to be added to that long list of successful pilots soaring the universe with the LORD. The best pilots have a Heart to Fly. They continue to be lifelong intercessory prayer warriors and students of the Word. They never feel they know enough about flying. When interviewed, they are likely to say, the more I know, the more I know—I know very little. They are constantly aware of GOD's vastness and their state of grace through JESUS CHRIST. They Fly in constant humility. They rely on GOD's instruments versus any natural instinct. They recognize their human frailties.

---

[327] Galatians 5:22-23 (MSG)

[328] 1 Samuel 13

[329] 2 Kings 20

[330] Book of Ruth

[331] Acts 13-28

Chapter 22: Your Engine "the Heart"

These pilots receive the weather reports second-by-second. They wake-up making sure to have quality fellowship with JESUS. They check-in often during the day to get the best flight path data. They adjust their direction based on the information received from the HOLY SPIRIT. They realize that their life depends on quick responses to external and internal forces.

So finally, I'm asking you to **not** watch the gas gauge in order to soar. To learn from:

- Elisha's servant that more are with you than against you
- Queen Esther that fasting and praying can save a nation
- Apostle Paul that blindness is the beginning of real sight
- Joseph that the pit can lead you straight to the palace
- Sarah that you are never too old to receive GOD's promise
- Moses that having a police record does not disqualify you
- King David that you are never too young to become a leader
- Prophetess Deborah that women can do anything
- Rahab that your past does not define your future
- Peter that failure can lead to forgiveness
- and most importantly from JESUS CHRIST that greater is HE that is in you than HE that is in the world, giving you a guarantee to do *greater works*[332].

I would like to end this book with the inscription on the Wright Memorial erected at Kitty Hawk and dedicated in 1932. I believe it says why you are meant to Fly. Are you willing to put your name on it?

IN COMMEMORATION OF THE CONQUEST OF THE AIR BY THE BROTHERS WILBUR AND ORVILLE WRIGHT. CONCEIVED BY GENIUS, AND ACHIEVED BY DAUNTLESS RESOLUTION AND UNCONQUERABLE FAITH.

---

[332] John 14:12

Fly With GOD

Dear LORD,

Open my heart and give me the courage to do YOUR will.

Open my heart and give me the courage to do YOUR will.

Open my heart and give me the courage to do YOUR will.

In JESUS' name, I pray.

Meditation Scriptures

- *Ephesians 6:6 (KJV):Not with eyeservice, as menpleasers; but as the servants of CHRIST, doing the will of GOD from the heart*

Bonus Exercises: Meditate On These Scriptures

Summing it all up, friends, I'd say you'll do best by filling your minds and meditating on things true, noble, reputable, authentic, compelling, gracious—the best, not the worst; the beautiful, not the ugly; things to praise, not things to curse. Put into practice what you learned from me, what you heard and saw and realized. Do that, and God, who makes everything work together, will work you into his most excellent harmonies.

Philippians 4:8-9 (The Message)

This book led us to the heart of our issues. Flying with GOD has always been about a clean heart – the key to flying. Remember Flying with GOD is not an event but a journey. Let HIM lead.

Meditate on these scriptures. Ask GOD to speak to your heart and select the scriptures HE has for you. Don't move to the next scripture until you have something to write about even if it takes days for you to release your thoughts.

Psalm 7:9 KJV Oh let the wickedness of the wicked come to an end; but establish the just: for the righteous GOD trieth the hearts and reins.

Psalm 10:17 KJV LORD, thou hast heard the desire of the humble: thou wilt prepare their heart, thou wilt cause thine ear to hear:

Fly With GOD

Psalm 17:3 NIV Though you probe my heart and examine me at night, though you test me, you will find nothing; I have resolved that my mouth will not sin.

Psalm 19:14 KJV Let the words of my mouth, and the meditation of my heart, be acceptable in thy sight, O LORD, my strength, and my redeemer.

Psalm 119:31-33 KJV I have stuck unto thy testimonies: O LORD, put me not to shame. I will run the way of thy commandments, when thou shalt enlarge my heart. Teach me, O LORD, the way of thy statutes; and I shall keep it unto the end.

Jeremiah 17:10 KJV I the LORD search the heart, I try the reins, even to give every man according to his ways, and according to the fruit of his doings.

Matthew 5:8 KJV Blessed are the pure in heart: for they shall see GOD.

Bonus Exercises: Meditate On These Scriptures

> *Mark 12:30 KJV And thou shalt love the LORD thy GOD with all thy heart, and with all thy soul, and with all thy mind, and with all thy strength: this is the first commandment.*

> *Luke 8:15 KJV But that on the good ground are they, which in an honest and good heart, having heard the word, keep it, and bring forth fruit with patience.*

> *Luke 10:27 KJV And he answering said, Thou shalt love the LORD thy GOD with all thy heart, and with all thy soul, and with all thy strength, and with all thy mind; and thy neighbour as thyself.*

> *Luke 12:34 KJV For where your treasure is, there will your heart be also.*

Fly With GOD

> *Romans 8:26-28 KJV In the same way, the Spirit helps us in our weakness. We do not know what we ought to pray for, but the Spirit himself intercedes for us with groans that words cannot express. And he who searches our hearts knows the mind of the Spirit, because the Spirit intercedes for the saints in accordance with GOD's will. And we know that in all things GOD works for the good of those who love him, who have been called according to his purpose.*

> *1 Corinthians 2:9 KJV But as it is written, Eye hath not seen, nor ear heard, neither have entered into the heart of man, the things which GOD hath prepared for them that love him.*

> *2 Corinthians 1:21-22 NIV Now it is GOD who makes both us and you stand firm in CHRIST. HE anointed us, set his seal of ownership on us, and put his Spirit in our hearts as a deposit, guaranteeing what is to come.*

> *2 Corinthians 4:6 KJV For GOD, who commanded the light to shine out of darkness, hath shined in our hearts, to give the light of the knowledge of the glory of GOD in the face of JESUS CHRIST.*

2 Corinthians 9:7 KJV Every man according as he purposeth in his heart, so let him give; not grudgingly, or of necessity: for GOD loveth a cheerful giver.

Ephesians 3:17-21 KJV That CHRIST may dwell in your hearts by faith; that ye, being rooted and grounded in love, May be able to comprehend with all saints what is the breadth, and length, and depth, and height; And to know the love of CHRIST, which passeth knowledge, that ye might be filled with all the fulness of GOD. Now unto him that is able to do exceeding abundantly above all that we ask or think, according to the power that worketh in us, Unto him be glory in the church by CHRIST JESUS throughout all ages, world without end. Amen.

Ephesians 5:19 KJV Speaking to yourselves in psalms and hymns and spiritual songs, singing and making melody in your heart to the LORD;

Philippians 4:7 And the peace of GOD, which passeth all understanding, shall keep your hearts and minds through CHRIST JESUS.

Fly With GOD

> *Hebrews 4:12 KJV For the word of GOD is quick, and powerful, and sharper than any two-edged sword, piercing even to the dividing asunder of soul and spirit, and of the joints and marrow, and is a discerner of the thoughts and intents of the heart.*

> *1 Peter 3:14-17 NIV But even if you should suffer for what is right, you are blessed. "Do not fear what they fear; do not be frightened. But in your hearts set apart CHRIST as LORD. Always be prepared to give an answer to everyone who asks you to give the reason for the hope that you have. But do this with gentleness and respect, keeping a clear conscience, so that those who speak maliciously against your good behavior in CHRIST may be ashamed of their slander. It is better, if it is GOD's will, to suffer for doing good than for doing evil.*

> *John 3:18-22 NIV Dear children, let us not love with words or tongue but with actions and in truth. This then is how we know that we belong to the truth, and how we set our hearts at rest in his presence whenever our hearts condemn us. For GOD is greater than our hearts, and HE knows everything. Dear friends, if our hearts do not condemn us, we have confidence before GOD and receive from him anything we ask, because we obey his commands and do what pleases him.*

About the Author

As the CEO of Build-IT-Up, LLC Lily builds relationships and creates strategic alliances in the Federal and Private sectors by helping people make "real" connections. Lily has consistently been a catalyst for change in her clients' professional and personal lives. As a mentor, coach, speaker, trainer, consultant, and author, Ms. Milliner is widely recognized for her creative and inspirational presentations having trained thousands of individuals throughout the U.S. and the Caribbean. As a Talk Show Host – she created, and produced "What's Your Story", where she interviewed writers crossing every industry; from the traditional print media to the folks who helped build the billion dollar video gaming industry. Ms. Milliner is also the proud recipient of the Historically Underutilized Business Zones Contractors National Council Employee of the Year Award. Not content to sit on the sideline's Lily now turns her attention to the Self-Help Industry which she believes is ripe for a paradigm shift.

www.LilySpeaks.com

Twitter   Facebook   Instagram